Succeed in
Cambridge English:
Proficiency

Certificate of Proficiency in English (CPE)

Practice Tests

Andrew Betsis
Sean Haughton
Lawrence Mamas

GlobalELT

Introduction

Cambridge English: Proficiency is a high-level qualification, at Level **C2**, the highest level of the CEFR scale, that is globally recognised by companies, universities and governments. It is intended for people who want to achieve exceptional ability with English in order to study at university or seek jobs at senior management level in international business settings. The **Cambridge English: Proficiency** certificate is a proof of your ability to use English at the highest levels of academic and professional life approaching that of a native speaker.

The test consists of four papers, Reading, Writing, Listening and Speaking, and it tests all areas of language ability. The new 2013 format of the exam is shorter than the previous examination by approximately 2 hours. Each of the four papers carries 25% of the total marks.

The **Succeed in Cambridge English: Proficiency** book consists of **8 Complete Practice Tests** for the new **2013 exam format** which aim to help students acquire all the necessary skills needed to pass the **Cambridge English: Proficiency** exam.

Published by GLOBAL ELT LTD
Brighton, East Sussex
www.globalelt.co.uk
Copyright © **GLOBAL ELT LTD 2012**

British Library Cataloguing-in-Publication Data

A catalogue record of this book is available from the British Library.
● Succeed in CPE - 8 Practice Tests - Student's Book - ISBN: 978-1-904663-07-2
● Succeed in CPE - 8 Practice Tests - Teacher's Book - ISBN: 978-1-904663-08-9

The authors and publishers wish to acknowledge the following use of material:
The photos in the Speaking Section Testss 1- 8 © Ingram Publishing Image Library - © www.123rf.com Image Library

CONTENTS

Cambridge English: Proficiency Revised 2013 Format

Paper	Time	Questions	Task Types	Test Focus
Paper 1 Reading	• 1 hour 30 min	• 53 questions • 7 parts	**Part 1** - Multiple-choice cloze - 8 questions **Part 2** - Open cloze - 8 questions **Part 3** - Word formation - 8 questions **Part 4** - Key word transformations - 6 questions **Part 5** - A text followed by 4-option multiple-choice questions - 6 questions **Part 6** - gapped text task – paragraphs removed - 7 questions **Part 7** - multiple matching - one or several short texts preceded by multiple-matching questions - 10 questions	**Part 1** - vocabulary **Part 2** - grammar and vocabulary **Part 3** - vocabulary and word formation **Part 4** - grammar and vocabulary **Part 5** - specific information, detail, opinion and attitude **Part 6** - text structure and also cohesion and coherence **Part 7** - specific information, detail, opinion, attitude
Paper 2 Writing	• 1 hour 30 min	• 2 parts: essay, article, report, letter, review	**Part 1** - compulsory task: discursive essay (240–280 words) - essay based on two texts of 100 words each **Part 2** - one task from a choice of five (280-320 words in total). The task types can be: essay, article, letter, review or report. **Questions 2-4** candidates are provided with a context, topic, purpose and target reader for their piece of writing. In **Question 5** candidates can choose one of two tasks based on the set reading texts.	**Part 1** – summarising and evaluating the key ideas of the texts provided as input **Part 2** – candidates have to put together and develop their ideas on a topic with a purpose for writing and a target reader in mind and use appropriate language for each task type
Paper 3 Listening	• 40 minutes • 30 questions	• 4 parts **Task types:** multiple choice, sentence completion, multiple matching	**Part 1** - multiple choice – three short unrelated extracts; exchanges between interacting speakers or monologues; two questions per text - 6 questions **Part 2** - sentence completion – a monologue - 9 questions **Part 3** - multiple choice – a conversation between interacting speakers - 5 questions **Part 4** - multiple matching - five short themed monologues. Two tasks; each task requires selection of the correct option from a list of eight options - 10 questions All texts will be heard twice.	**Part 1** - attitude, opinion, purpose, function, agreement between speakers, course of action, general gist, detail, etc. **Part 2** - stated opinion and specific information **Part 3** - attitude and opinion **Part 4** - gist, attitude, main points, interpreting context
Paper 4 Speaking	• 16 minutes	• 3 parts	**Part 1** - conversation between the interlocutor and each candidate (spoken questions) - 2 minutes **Part 2** - decision-making task based on written and visual stimuli; 2-way conversation - 4 minutes **Part 3** - a long turn by each candidate, followed by a discussion on topics related to the long turns - 10 minutes	**Part 1** - general interactional and social language **Part 2** - agreeing and/or disagreeing, suggesting, speculating, evaluating etc.; comparing, describing, expressing opinions and speculating, sustaining an interaction, exchanging ideas **Part 3** - expressing and justifying opinions, organising a larger unit of discourse

Cambridge English: Proficiency Format

Cambridge English: Proficiency

Paper 4
Speaking
Section

Tests: 1 - 8

Speaking Section

Paper 4: SPEAKING
Time: 16 minutes per pair of candidates

Students take the Speaking test in pairs (occasionally, where there is an uneven number of candidates, three students may be required to take the test together). There are two examiners (an assessor and an interlocutor) and one of them (the assessor) does not take part in the interaction but assesses your performance according to four analytical scales. The other examiner (the interlocutor) conducts the test and tells you what you have to do. The interlocutor also gives you a global mark for your performance in the test as a whole.

| Paper 4 Speaking | PART 1 | (2 minutes / 3 minutes for groups of three) |

In **Part 1** of the Speaking test, you may be asked to talk about your interests, general experiences, studies or career, and plans for the future. The examiner will first ask you for some general information about yourself, and then widen the scope of the conversation to include subjects like leisure activities, studies, travel, holiday experiences and daily life. Respond directly to the examiner's questions, avoid very short answers, and listen when your partner is speaking. You are not required to interact with your partner in this part, but you may do so if you wish.

Interlocutor: Good morning/afternoon/evening. My name is .... and this is my colleague .... And your names are .... ? Could I have your mark sheets, please?   Thank you.

First of all, we'd like to know something about you.
Where are you from (Candidate A)? And you (Candidate B)?
[address Candidate B] Are you working or studying at the moment?
[address Candidate A] And you?

Select a further question for each candidate:
- You said you were from *[place name]*. What do you enjoy about living there?
  Are there any improvements that could be made? Would you consider living elsewhere?
- How much time do you spend studying/working a day?
- What do you like to do in your spare time?
- What do you see yourself doing in ten years' time?
- Do you have a mobile phone? How important is it for you?

Candidates: ....
Interlocutor: Thank you.

| Paper 4 Speaking | PART 2 | (approximately 4 minutes / 6 minutes for groups of three) |

| TV documentary - Impact of technology on people |

Now, in this part of the test you're going to do something together. Here are some pictures of people in different situations.

Place Part 2 booklet, open at Task 1, in front of the candidates. Select two of the pictures for the candidates to look at.

First, I'd like you to look at pictures * and * and talk together about how technology has affected humanity.

You have about a minute for this, so don't worry if I interrupt you. *(2 minutes for groups of three)*

Candidates *1 minute*
(2 minutes for groups of three):   ....
Interlocutor: Thank you.

I'd like you to imagine that a television documentary is being produced on the impact technology has had on human beings as a species. These pictures show some ideas that have been presented.

After discussing the pictures, I would like you to decide which idea would be most interesting to develop for the show. You have about three minutes to talk about this. *(4 minutes for groups of three)*

Candidates: *3 minutes*
(4 minutes for groups of three):   ....
Interlocutor: Thank you. (Can I have the booklet, please?) [Retrieve Part 2 booklet.]

TV documentary - Impact of technology on people

A

B

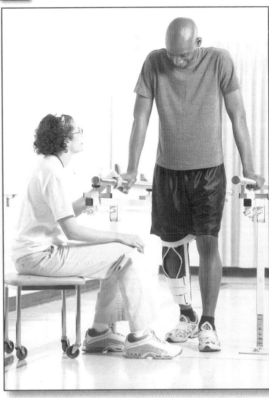

C

D

Speaking Section

Interlocutor: Now, in this part of the test you're each going to talk on your own for about two minutes. You need to listen while your partner is speaking because you'll be asked to comment afterwards.

So (Candidate A), I'm going to give you a card with a question written on it and I'd like you to tell us what you think. There are also some ideas on the card for you to use if you like. All right? Here is your card.
Place Part 3 booklet, open at Task 1 (a), in front of Candidate A.

Please let (Candidate B) see your card. Remember (Candidate A), you have about 2 minutes to talk before we join in.
[Allow up to 10 seconds before saying, if necessary: Would you like to begin now?]

Task 1(a):

> What is the best way to learn a new language?
> - lessons
> - reading for pleasure
> - living in the country of your chosen language

Candidate A (2 minutes):   .... **Interlocutor:** Thank you.

Interlocutor: *Ask one of the following questions to Candidate B:*
- What do you find to be the best way to learn foreign languages?
- Are there any other ways you can think of to help in learning a foreign language?
- Do you think you are good at learning foreign languages?

> *Invite Candidate A to join in by selecting one of the following prompts:*
> - What do you think?
> - Do you agree?
> - How about you?

Candidates (1 minute):   .... **Interlocutor:** Thank you. (Can I have the booklet, please?) *Retrieve Part 3 booklet.*

Interlocutor: Now (Candidate B), it's your turn to be given a question. Here is your card.
Place Part 3 booklet, open at Task 1 (b), in front of Candidate B.

Task 1(b):

> Why do people learn new languages?
> - travel
> - knowledge
> - careers

Please let (Candidate A) see your card. Remember (Candidate B), you have about two minutes to tell us what you think, and there are some ideas on the card for you to use if you like. All right?
[Allow up to 10 seconds before saying, if necessary: Would you like to begin now?]

Candidate B (2 minutes):   .... **Interlocutor:** Thank you

Interlocutor: *Ask one of the following questions to Candidate A.*
- Do you think people would be more successful language students if they didn't have to sit exams?
- What is the best motivator in learning another language?
- To what extent is language ability natural?

> *Invite Candidate B to join in by selecting one of the following prompts:*
> - What do you think?
> - Do you agree?
> - How about you?

Candidates (1 minute):   .... **Interlocutor:** Thank you

Interlocutor: Now, to finish the test, we're going to talk about 'language learning' in general.
(up to 4 minutes) Address a selection of the following questions to both candidates:

- In what kind of job do you need to be able to speak another language?
- Do you use a language other than your own on a daily basis for purposes other than study?
- What are the disadvantages of learning another language?
- How many languages do you think it would be possible for one person to learn?
- Can you think of ways in which to test foreign language ability other than through examinations?

Candidates (4 min):   .... **Interlocutor:** Thank you. That is the end of the test.

TEST 2

Paper 4: SPEAKING
Time: 16 minutes per pair of candidates

Students take the Speaking test in pairs (occasionally, where there is an uneven number of candidates, three students may be required to take the test together). There are two examiners (an assessor and an interlocutor) and one of them (the assessor) does not take part in the interaction but assesses your performance according to four analytical scales. The other examiner (the interlocutor) conducts the test and tells you what you have to do. The interlocutor also gives you a global mark for your performance in the test as a whole.

| Paper 4 Speaking | PART 1 | (2 minutes / 3 minutes for groups of three) |

In **Part 1** of the Speaking test, you may be asked to talk about your interests, general experiences, studies or career, and plans for the future. The examiner will first ask you for some general information about yourself, and then widen the scope of the conversation to include subjects like leisure activities, studies, travel, holiday experiences and daily life. Respond directly to the examiner's questions, avoid very short answers, and listen when your partner is speaking. You are not required to interact with your partner in this part, but you may do so if you wish.

Interlocutor: Good morning/afternoon/evening. My name is .... and this is my colleague ....
And your names are .... ? Could I have your mark sheets, please? Thank you.

First of all, we'd like to know something about you.
Where are you from (Candidate A)? And you (Candidate B)?
[address Candidate B] Are you working or studying at the moment?
[address Candidate A] And you?

Select a further question for each candidate:
● Where are you from?
● What do you do?
● How long have you been studying English?
● What do you enjoy most about learning English?
● Why did you decide to start learning English?

Candidates: ....
Interlocutor: Thank you.

| Paper 4 Speaking | PART 2 | (approximately 4 minutes / 6 minutes for groups of three) |

Spending time outdoors - Ways that outdoor spaces can be used

Now, in this part of the test you're going to do something together. Here are some pictures of people in different situations.

Place Part 2 booklet, open at Task 1, in front of the candidates. Select two of the pictures for the candidates to look at.

First, I'd like you to look at pictures * and * and talk together about how different people enjoy spending time outdoors.

You have about a minute for this, so don't worry if I interrupt you. *(2 minutes for groups of three)*

Candidates *1 minute*
(2 minutes for groups of three):   ....
Interlocutor: Thank you.

I'd like you to imagine that a book is being written about the different ways that outdoor spaces can be used. These pictures show some ideas that are being considered for the book.
You have about three minutes to talk about this. *(4 minutes for groups of three)*

Candidates: *3 minutes*
(4 minutes for groups of three):   ....
Interlocutor: Thank you. (Can I have the booklet, please?) [Retrieve Part 2 booklet.]

Speaking Section

Spending time outdoors - Ways that outdoor spaces can be used

A

B

C

D

Paper 4 Speaking   **PART 3**   (approximately 10 minutes)   **The environment**

Now, in this part of the test you're each going to talk on your own for about two minutes. You need to listen while your partner is speaking because you will be asked to comment afterwards.

So (Candidate A), I'm going to give you a card with a question written on it and I'd like you to tell us what you think. There are also some ideas on the card for you to use if you like. All right? Here is your card.
Place Part 3 booklet, open at Task 1(a), in front of Candidate A.

Please let (Candidate B) see your card. Remember (Candidate A), you have about 2 minutes to talk before we join.

Task 1(a): | What is the best way to enjoy the great outdoors?
- sport
- art
- holidays

Candidate A (2 minutes):   .... **Interlocutor:** Thank you.

Interlocutor: *Ask one of the following questions to Candidate B:*
- Do enjoy doing everyday activities such as reading outdoors?
- Which do you prefer – playing sport outdoors or indoors?
- Can you think of any other ways in which we could fully enjoy the great outdoors?

> Invite Candidate A to join in by selecting one of the following prompts:
> - What do you think?
> - Do you agree?
> - How about you?

Candidates (1 minute): .... **Interlocutor:** Thank you. (Can I have the booklet, please?) *Retrieve Part 3 booklet.*

Interlocutor: Now (Candidate B), it's your turn to be given a question. Here is your card.
Place Part 3 booklet, open at Task 1(b), in front of Candidate B.

Task 1(b): | Do you think that if people have a stronger relationship with the countryside that they will take better care of it?
- education
- conservation
- recycling

Please let (Candidate A) see your card. Remember (Candidate B), you have about two minutes to tell us what you think, and there are some ideas on the card for you to use if you like. All right?
[Allow up to 10 seconds before saying, if necessary: Would you like to begin now?]

Candidate B (2 minutes):   .... **Interlocutor:** Thank you

Interlocutor: *Ask one of the following questions to Candidate A.*
- What do you think would be the best way to encourage people to look after the environment?
- What would be the best motivator in protecting the environment?
- To what extent is this about education?

> Invite Candidate B to join in by selecting one of the following prompts:
> - What do you think?
> - Do you agree?
> - How about you?

Candidates (1 minute): ....   **Interlocutor:**   Thank you

Interlocutor: Now, to finish the test, we're going to talk about the environment and human relationships with the
(up to 4 minutes) environment in general.

Address a selection of the following questions to both candidates:
- What is the most important problem with regards to the environment?
- How could we alter our lives to be more environmentally friendly?
- What could the government do to help protect the environment?
- What could businesses do to help with the conservation of nature?
- Do you think that people's attitudes towards the environment alter with age – are young people, for example, more caring?

Candidates (4 min):   .... **Interlocutor:** Thank you. That is the end of the test.

TEST 3

Speaking Section

Paper 4: SPEAKING
Time: 16 minutes per pair of candidates

Students take the Speaking test in pairs (occasionally, where there is an uneven number of candidates, three students may be required to take the test together). There are two examiners (an assessor and an interlocutor) and one of them (the assessor) does not take part in the interaction but assesses your performance according to four analytical scales. The other examiner (the interlocutor) conducts the test and tells you what you have to do. The interlocutor also gives you a global mark for your performance in the test as a whole.

Paper 4 Speaking	PART 1	(2 minutes / 3 minutes for groups of three)

In **Part 1** of the Speaking test, you may be asked to talk about your interests, general experiences, studies or career, and plans for the future. The examiner will first ask you for some general information about yourself, and then widen the scope of the conversation to include subjects like leisure activities, studies, travel, holiday experiences and daily life. Respond directly to the examiner's questions, avoid very short answers, and listen when your partner is speaking. You are not required to interact with your partner in this part, but you may do so if you wish.

Interlocutor: Good morning/afternoon/evening. My name is .... and this is my colleague ....
And your names are .... ? Could I have your mark sheets, please?   Thank you.

First of all, we'd like to know something about you.
Where are you from (Candidate A)? And you (Candidate B)?
[address Candidate B] Are you working or studying at the moment?
[address Candidate A] And you?

Select a further question for each candidate:
● With whom do you prefer to travel? ...(Why?)
● Are you more fond of long or short distance travel?
● What has been your most exciting travel experience thus far?
● Name some things that you would never leave behind you when you travel.
● Do you like adventure holidays or you prefer to lie on a beach for hours?

Candidates: ....
Interlocutor: Thank you.

Paper 4 Speaking	PART 2	(approximately 4 minutes / 6 minutes for groups of three)

Technology in medicine - working in a hospital

Now, in this part of the test you're going to do something together. Here are some pictures of people in different situations.

Place Part 2 booklet, open at Task 1, in front of the candidates. Select two of the pictures for the candidates to look at.

First, I'd like you to look at pictures * and * and about talk how modern technology has helped doctors to develop new treatments.

You have about a minute for this, so don't worry if I interrupt you. *(2 minutes for groups of three)*

Candidates *1 minute*
(2 minutes for groups of three):   ....
Interlocutor: Thank you.

I'd like you to imagine that a television documentary is being produced on working in a hospital. These pictures show some of the issues that are being considered.

Talk together about how the different issues related to working in a hospital that these pictures show. Then decide which issue might provoke more interest.

You have about three minutes to talk about this. *(4 minutes for groups of three)*

Candidates: *3 minutes*
(4 minutes for groups of three):   ....
Interlocutor: Thank you. (Can I have the booklet, please?) [Retrieve Part 2 booklet.]

A

Technology in medicine - working in a hospital

B

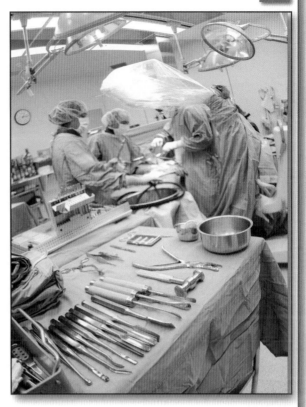

C

D

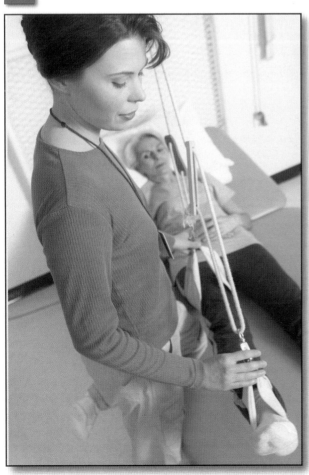

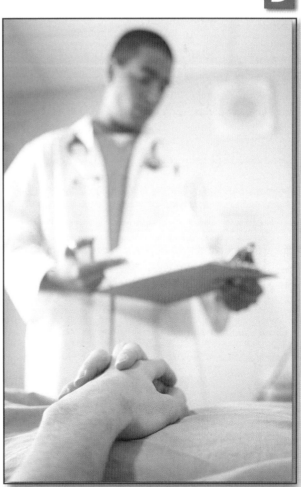

Speaking Section

Paper 4 Speaking   **PART 3**   (approximately 10 minutes)   **Living alone**

Speaking Section

Interlocutor: Now, in this part of the test you're each going to talk on your own for about two minutes. You need to listen while your partner is speaking because you'll be asked to comment afterwards.

So *(Candidate A)*, I'm going to give you a card with a question written on it and I'd like you to tell us what you think. There are also some ideas on the card for you to use if you like. All right? Here is your card.
Place Part 3 booklet, open at Task 1(a), in front of Candidate A.

Please let *(Candidate B)* see your card. Remember *(Candidate A)*, you have about 2 minutes to talk before we join in.
[Allow up to 10 seconds before saying, if necessary: Would you like to begin now?]

Task 1(a):

> Which is preferable, being independent and free,
> or having the security of your family around you?
> - at different ages
> - growth
> - love

Candidate A (2 minutes): ....   **Interlocutor:** Thank you.

Interlocutor: *Ask one of the following questions to Candidate B:*
- On the whole, would you say you were an independent person?
- Do you think it's better to live alone or with family?

> *Invite Candidate A to join in by selecting one of the following prompts:*
> - What do you think?
> - Do you agree?
> - How about you?

Candidates (1 minute): ....   **Interlocutor:** Thank you. (Can I have the booklet, please?) *Retrieve Part 3 booklet.*

Interlocutor: Now *(Candidate B)*, it's your turn to be given a question. Here is your card.
Place Part 3 booklet, open at Task 1(b), in front of Candidate B.

Task 1(b):

> Why do you think more people live alone now?
> - work commitments
> - wealth
> - values

Please let *(Candidate A)* see your card. Remember *(Candidate B)*, you have about two minutes to tell us what you think, and there are some ideas on the card for you to use if you like. All right?
[Allow up to 10 seconds before saying, if necessary: Would you like to begin now?]

Candidate B (2 minutes):   ....   **Interlocutor:** Thank you

Interlocutor: *Ask one of the following questions to Candidate A.*
- Do you think fewer people will live alone in the future?
- Would you prefer to live alone or with somebody?

> *Invite Candidate B to join in by selecting one of the following prompts:*
> - What do you think?
> - Do you agree?
> - How about you?

Candidates (1 minute): ....   **Interlocutor:** Thank you

Interlocutor: Now, to finish the test, we're going to talk about living arrangements in general.
(up to 4 minutes) Address a selection of the following questions to both candidates:

- Do you think living arrangements have changed in your country in the last few decades?
- To what extent are some changes related to the changing nature of the family?
- How do you think living arrangements might change in the future?
- Do you think the structure of the family is as tight as it was?
- What do you think might happen to the structure of the family in the future?

Candidates (4 min):   ....   **Interlocutor:** Thank you. That is the end of the test.

TEST 4

Paper 4: SPEAKING
Time: 16 minutes per pair of candidates

Students take the Speaking test in pairs (occasionally, where there is an uneven number of candidates, three students may be required to take the test together). There are two examiners (an assessor and an interlocutor) and one of them (the assessor) does not take part in the interaction but assesses your performance according to four analytical scales. The other examiner (the interlocutor) conducts the test and tells you what you have to do. The interlocutor also gives you a global mark for your performance in the test as a whole.

Paper 4 Speaking   PART 1   (2 minutes / 3 minutes for groups of three)

In **Part 1** of the Speaking test, you may be asked to talk about your interests, general experiences, studies or career, and plans for the future. The examiner will first ask you for some general information about yourself, and then widen the scope of the conversation to include subjects like leisure activities, studies, travel, holiday experiences and daily life. Respond directly to the examiner's questions, avoid very short answers, and listen when your partner is speaking. You are not required to interact with your partner in this part, but you may do so if you wish.

Interlocutor: Good morning/afternoon/evening. My name is .... and this is my colleague ....
And your names are .... ? Could I have your mark sheets, please?   Thank you.

First of all, we'd like to know something about you.
Where are you from (Candidate A)? And you (Candidate B)?
[address Candidate B] Are you working or studying at the moment?
[address Candidate A] And you?

Select a further question for each candidate:
- What do you enjoy best about the area in which you live?
- How difficult would it be for you to have to move to a new neighbourhood?
- What, from your perspective, is the most interesting aspect of learning to speak English?
- Do you have to travel far every day to work / place of study?
- Do you think it is easy for young people nowadays to find a job?
- In the future, do you see yourself living in your own country or do you have aspirations to live abroad?

Candidates: ....
Interlocutor: Thank you.

Paper 4 Speaking   PART 2   (approximately 4 minutes / 6 minutes for groups of three)

Magazine Article – Natural Threats

Now, in this part of the test you're going to do something together. Here are some pictures of people in different situations.

Place Part 2 booklet, open at Task 1, in front of the candidates. Select two of the pictures for the candidates to look at.

First, I'd like you to look at pictures * and * and talk together about which picture interests you more.

You have about a minute for this, so don't worry if I interrupt you. *(2 minutes for groups of three)*

Candidates *1 minute*
(2 minutes for groups of three):   ....
Interlocutor: Thank you.

I'd like you to imagine that a magazine is planning a feature on Dangers of the Natural World. These pictures will be used to accompany the article.

Talk together about the types of natural threats humans have to deal with, in relation to the pictures shown. Then suggest one other type of threat that could be included in the feature.

You have about three minutes to talk about this (4 minutes for groups of three).

Candidates: *3 minutes*
(4 minutes for groups of three):   ....
Interlocutor: Thank you. (Can I have the booklet, please?) [Retrieve Part 2 booklet.]

Speaking Section

Magazine Article – Natural Threats

Paper 4 Speaking   **PART 3**   (approximately 10 minutes)   Success in life

Now, in this part of the test you're each going to talk on your own for about two minutes. You need to listen while your partner is speaking because you will be asked to comment afterwards.

So (Candidate A), I'm going to give you a card with a question written on it and I'd like you to tell us what you think. There are also some ideas on the card for you to use if you like. All right? Here is your card.
Place Part 3 booklet, open at Task 1(a), in front of Candidate A.

Please let (Candidate B) see your card. Remember (Candidate A), you have about 2 minutes to talk before we join.

Task 1(a):
| What is the key to success in life? |
| • Friends and family |
| • Money |
| • Job satisfaction |

Candidate A (2 minutes):   .... Interlocutor: Thank you.

Interlocutor: *Ask one of the following questions to Candidate B:*
- Is there such a thing as an ideal job?
- Are there more benefits or drawbacks to coming from a big family?
- What would you do with the rest of your life if you had all the money you needed and never had to work again?

Invite Candidate A to join in by selecting one of the following prompts:
- What do you think?
- Do you agree?
- How about you?

Candidates (1 minute): .... Interlocutor: Thank you. (Can I have the booklet, please?) *Retrieve Part 3 booklet.*

Interlocutor: Now (Candidate B), it's your turn to be given a question. Here is your card.
Place Part 3 booklet, open at Task 1(b), in front of Candidate B.

Task 1(b):
| Why are some athletes more successful than others? |
| • Genes |
| • Motivation |
| • Funding and facilities |

Please let (Candidate A) see your card. Remember (Candidate B), you have about two minutes to tell us what you think, and there are some ideas on the card for you to use if you like. All right?
[Allow up to 10 seconds before saying, if necessary: Would you like to begin now?]
Candidate B (2 minutes):   .... Interlocutor: Thank you

Interlocutor: *Ask one of the following questions to Candidate A.*
- Do you think there is a drugs problem in sport today?
- How would you better support athletes if you were the Minister for Sport?
- Do you think it is possible to be a successful athlete without receiving financial help from the government or sponsors?

Invite Candidate B to join in by selecting one of the following prompts:
- What do you think?
- Do you agree?
- How about you?

Candidates (1 minute): .... Interlocutor: Thank you

Interlocutor: Now, to finish the test, we're going to talk about success in general.
(up to 4 minutes) Address a selection of the following questions to both candidates:

- To what extent do you agree that hard work is the key to success?
- What personality skills do people need to maximise their success in life?
- Cheating seems to be a big problem in sport today. Why do you think that is?
- Is it easier for someone from a wealthy background to become a success than for someone who comes from a working class family?
- Success is defined as how many friends you have and how much money you earn. Would you agree?
- Celebrities are great role models for those who want to be a success. Would you agree?

Candidates (4 min):   .... Interlocutor: Thank you. That is the end of the test.

TEST 5

Speaking Section

Paper 4: SPEAKING
Time: 16 minutes per pair of candidates

Students take the Speaking test in pairs (occasionally, where there is an uneven number of candidates, three students may be required to take the test together). There are two examiners (an assessor and an interlocutor) and one of them (the assessor) does not take part in the interaction but assesses your performance according to four analytical scales. The other examiner (the interlocutor) conducts the test and tells you what you have to do. The interlocutor also gives you a global mark for your performance in the test as a whole.

Paper 4 Speaking   **PART 1**   (2 minutes / 3 minutes for groups of three)

In **Part 1** of the Speaking test, you may be asked to talk about your interests, general experiences, studies or career, and plans for the future. The examiner will first ask you for some general information about yourself, and then widen the scope of the conversation to include subjects like leisure activities, studies, travel, holiday experiences and daily life. Respond directly to the examiner's questions, avoid very short answers, and listen when your partner is speaking. You are not required to interact with your partner in this part, but you may do so if you wish.

Interlocutor: Good morning/afternoon/evening. My name is .... and this is my colleague .... And your names are .... ? Could I have your mark sheets, please?   Thank you.

First of all, we'd like to know something about you.
Where are you from (Candidate A)? And you (Candidate B)?
[address Candidate B] Are you working or studying at the moment?
[address Candidate A] And you?

Select a further question for each candidate:
- Is English your main subject of study? (What other subjects…?)
- Do you prefer to study alone or in the company of friends?
- You said you're from … ; have you lived there a long time?
- What might attract a tourist to your area – I mean, what is there to see there?
- Do many tourists visit your area of [candidate's own country]? (What other areas are popular with tourists?)
- What about your interests – what kinds of things do you do in your free time?

Candidates: ....
Interlocutor: Thank you.

Paper 4 Speaking   **PART 2**   (approximately 4 minutes / 6 minutes for groups of three)

Gallery Exhibition - Careers

Now, in this part of the test you're going to do something together. Here are some pictures of people in different professions.

Place Part 2 booklet, open at Task 1, in front of the candidates. Select two of the pictures for the candidates to look at.

First, I'd like you to look at pictures * and * and talk together about the difficult and rewarding aspects of carrying out these jobs.

You have about a minute for this, so don't worry if I interrupt you. *(2 minutes for groups of three)*

Candidates *1 minute*
(2 minutes for groups of three):   ....
Interlocutor: Thank you.

I'd like you to imagine that a gallery is putting on an exhibition entitled *Everyday Heroes*.

Talk together about the contribution to society made by those in the professions featured in the pictures. Then decide which image would be most suitable as the main exhibit, which will be placed right in front of the entrance hallway.

You have about three minutes to talk about this *(4 minutes for groups of three).*

Candidates: *3 minutes*
(4 minutes for groups of three):   ....
Interlocutor: Thank you. (Can I have the booklet, please?) [Retrieve Part 2 booklet.]

Speaking Section

A

Gallery Exhibition - Careers

B

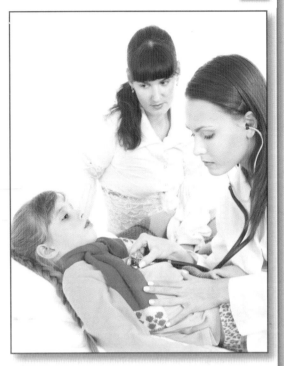

C

D

Speaking Section

Interlocutor: Now, in this part of the test you're each going to talk on your own for about two minutes. You need to listen while your partner is speaking because you'll be asked to comment afterwards.

So *(Candidate A)*, I'm going to give you a card with a question written on it and I'd like you to tell us what you think. There are also some ideas on the card for you to use if you like. All right? Here is your card.
Place Part 3 booklet, open at Task 1(a), in front of Candidate A.

Please let *(Candidate B)* see your card. Remember *(Candidate A)*, you have about 2 minutes to talk before we join in.
[Allow up to 10 seconds before saying, if necessary: Would you like to begin now?]

Task 1(a):
> What different types of 'rich person' are there?
> - inherited wealth
> - self-made
> - lucky

Candidate A (2 minutes): ....   **Interlocutor:** Thank you.

Interlocutor: *Ask one of the following questions to Candidate B:*
- Do you think people who make their own money are more deserving of respect?
- Do you ever play the lottery, and what is your general attitude to gambling?
- Do you think people who inherit their wealth appreciate it enough?

> *Invite Candidate A to join in by selecting one of the following prompts:*
> - What do you think?
> - Do you agree?
> - How about you?

Candidates (1 minute): ....   **Interlocutor:** Thank you. (Can I have the booklet, please?) *Retrieve Part 3 booklet.*

Interlocutor: Now *(Candidate B)*, it's your turn to be given a question. Here is your card.
Place Part 3 booklet, open at Task 1(b), in front of Candidate B.

Task 1(b):
> In what ways could wealthy people make a positive difference to the community with their resources?
> - charitable giving
> - investment in projects
> - sponsorship of youth

Please let *(Candidate A)* see your card. Remember *(Candidate B)*, you have about two minutes to tell us what you think, and there are some ideas on the card for you to use if you like. All right?
[Allow up to 10 seconds before saying, if necessary: Would you like to begin now?]

Candidate B (2 minutes):   ....   **Interlocutor:** Thank you

Interlocutor: *Ask one of the following questions to Candidate A.*
- Do charities make much of a difference through their work?
- What kinds of things should we invest in providing for poor areas of the country?
- What sorts of problems do young people in underprivileged areas face?

> Invite Candidate B to join in by selecting one of the following prompts:
> - What do you think?
> - Do you agree?
> - How about you?

Candidates (1 minute): ....   **Interlocutor:** Thank you

Interlocutor: Now, to finish the test, we're going to talk about living arrangements in general.
(up to 4 minutes) Address a selection of the following questions to both candidates:

- Is the gap between rich and poor narrowing?
- Why do some people become rich and successful while others remain poor?
- To what extent do we judge people based on their material possessions?
- Wealthy people are less likely to commit a crime than the poor are – do you agree?
- How can we make the world a more equitable place to live in?
- Is it greedy to keep a lot of money for and spend a lot of money on yourself?

Candidates (4 min): ....   **Interlocutor:** Thank you. That is the end of the test.

Paper 4: SPEAKING
Time: 16 minutes per pair of candidates

Students take the Speaking test in pairs (occasionally, where there is an uneven number of candidates, three students may be required to take the test together). There are two examiners (an assessor and an interlocutor) and one of them (the assessor) does not take part in the interaction but assesses your performance according to four analytical scales. The other examiner (the interlocutor) conducts the test and tells you what you have to do. The interlocutor also gives you a global mark for your performance in the test as a whole.

Paper 4 Speaking   PART 1   (2 minutes / 3 minutes for groups of three)

In **Part 1** of the Speaking test, you may be asked to talk about your interests, general experiences, studies or career, and plans for the future. The examiner will first ask you for some general information about yourself, and then widen the scope of the conversation to include subjects like leisure activities, studies, travel, holiday experiences and daily life. Respond directly to the examiner's questions, avoid very short answers, and listen when your partner is speaking. You are not required to interact with your partner in this part, but you may do so if you wish.

Interlocutor: Good morning/afternoon/evening. My name is .... and this is my colleague .... And your names are .... ? Could I have your mark sheets, please?   Thank you.

First of all, we'd like to know something about you.
Where are you from (Candidate A)? And you (Candidate B)?
[address Candidate B] Are you working or studying at the moment?
[address Candidate A] And you?

Select a further question for each candidate:
- What do you look forward to doing most when you go home at the end of each day?
- How are you with computers and technology?
- How important is it to establish a routine for yourself when you are working or studying?
- Could you tell us something about your taste in music?
- What about your eating habits – what are your favourite foods?
- How important is it to speak a foreign language in your country?

Candidates: ....
Interlocutor: Thank you.

Paper 4 Speaking   PART 2   (approximately 4 minutes / 6 minutes for groups of three)

Information booklet – Animal Cruelty

Now, in this part of the test you're going to do something together. Here are some pictures of animals in human care.

Place Part 2 booklet, open at Task 1, in front of the candidates. Select two of the pictures for the candidates to look at.

First, I'd like you to look at pictures * and * and talk together about what you can see happening and how this makes you feel. You have about a minute for this, so don't worry if I interrupt you. (*2 minutes for groups of three*)

Candidates *1 minute*
(2 minutes for groups of three):   ....
Interlocutor: Thank you.

I'd like you to imagine that the Society for the Prevention of Cruelty to Animals is choosing an image to feature on the front cover of its new information booklet, which will be sent to households all around the country as part of a new fundraising campaign.

Talk together about the ways in which humans mistreat animals, in relation to the pictures shown. Then decide which image would be most suitable to feature on the front cover of the information booklet.

You have about three minutes to talk about this (*4 minutes for groups of three*).

Candidates: *3 minutes*
(4 minutes for groups of three):   ....
Interlocutor: Thank you. (Can I have the booklet, please?) [Retrieve Part 2 booklet.]

Information booklet – Animal Cruelty

A

B

C

D

Speaking Section

Paper 4 Speaking   **PART 3**   (approximately 10 minutes) | Education |

Now, in this part of the test you're each going to talk on your own for about two minutes. You need to listen while your partner is speaking because you will be asked to comment afterwards.

So (*Candidate A*), I'm going to give you a card with a question written on it and I'd like you to tell us what you think. There are also some ideas on the card for you to use if you like. All right? Here is your card.
Place Part 3 booklet, open at Task 1(a), in front of Candidate A.

Please let (*Candidate B*) see your card. Remember (*Candidate A*), you have about 2 minutes to talk before we join.

Task 1(a):

> Why are some people unsuited to an academic-style education?
> ● health reasons
> ● behavioural reasons
> ● differing skill sets

Candidate A (2 minutes):   ....   **Interlocutor:** Thank you.

Interlocutor: *Ask one of the following questions to Candidate B:*
● Do you think those with mental disabilities should be sent to special schools?
● Why are some children better-behaved than others?
● What should schools do for young people who are not academically-minded?

> *Invite Candidate A to join in by selecting one of the following prompts:*
> ● What do you think?
> ● Do you agree?
> ● How about you?

Candidates (1 minute):   ....   **Interlocutor:** Thank you. (Can I have the booklet, please?) *Retrieve Part 3 booklet.*

Interlocutor: Now (*Candidate B*), it's your turn to be given a question. Here is your card.
Place Part 3 booklet, open at Task 1(b), in front of Candidate B.

Task 1(b):

> In what ways could the education system be improved?
> ● variety of subjects
> ● teaching methods
> ● facilities

Please let (*Candidate A*) see your card. Remember (*Candidate B*), you have about two minutes to tell us what you think, and there are some ideas on the card for you to use if you like. All right?
[Allow up to 10 seconds before saying, if necessary: Would you like to begin now?]

Candidate B (2 minutes):   ....   **Interlocutor:** Thank you

Interlocutor: *Ask one of the following questions to Candidate A.*
● What subjects should be added to the school curriculum?
● How do you rate the standard of teaching in schools in your country?
● Should sport play a big part in the school curriculum?

> *Invite Candidate B to join in by selecting one of the following prompts:*
> ● What do you think?
> ● Do you agree?
> ● How about you?

Candidates (1 minute): ....   **Interlocutor:**   Thank you

Interlocutor: Now, to finish the test, we're going to talk about success in general.
(*up to 4 minutes*) Address a selection of the following questions to both candidates:

● Does the education system favour the rich?
● What can be done to make our schools more effective learning centres?
● A degree is the minimum required qualification today – do you agree?
● Are early school-leavers doomed to work for life in poorly-paid jobs?
● The education you get on the streets is just as valuable as the one you get at school. What do you think of this statement?
● Do students who are not academically-minded benefit in any way from attending school?

Candidates (4 min):   ....   **Interlocutor:** Thank you. That is the end of the test.

TEST 7

Paper 4: SPEAKING
Time: 16 minutes per pair of candidates

Speaking Section

Students take the Speaking test in pairs (occasionally, where there is an uneven number of candidates, three students may be required to take the test together). There are two examiners (an assessor and an interlocutor) and one of them (the assessor) does not take part in the interaction but assesses your performance according to four analytical scales. The other examiner (the interlocutor) conducts the test and tells you what you have to do. The interlocutor also gives you a global mark for your performance in the test as a whole.

| Paper 4 Speaking | PART 1 | (2 minutes / 3 minutes for groups of three) |

In **Part 1** of the Speaking test, you may be asked to talk about your interests, general experiences, studies or career, and plans for the future. The examiner will first ask you for some general information about yourself, and then widen the scope of the conversation to include subjects like leisure activities, studies, travel, holiday experiences and daily life. Respond directly to the examiner's questions, avoid very short answers, and listen when your partner is speaking. You are not required to interact with your partner in this part, but you may do so if you wish.

Interlocutor: Good morning/afternoon/evening. My name is .... and this is my colleague .... And your names are .... ? Could I have your mark sheets, please?   Thank you.

First of all, we'd like to know something about you.
Where are you from (Candidate A)? And you (Candidate B)?
[address Candidate B] Are you working or studying at the moment?
[address Candidate A] And you?

Select a further question for each candidate:
- What sort of relationship do you have with the rest of your family?
- Is there anyone in particular in whom you confide when you have a problem you want to talk about?
- What is a typical day in the life of [candidate's name]?
- Are you interested in the Arts? (Do you often go to museums and galleries?)
- Do you take a keen interest in politics?
- What did you want to do with your life when you were a young child growing up? (Have things changed?)

Candidates: ....
Interlocutor: Thank you.

| Paper 4 Speaking | PART 2 | (approximately 4 minutes / 6 minutes for groups of three) |

Magazine Article – Group Behaviour

Now, in this part of the test you're going to do something together. Here are some pictures of people in groups.

Place Part 2 booklet, open at Task 1, in front of the candidates. Select two of the pictures for the candidates to look at.]

First, I'd like you to look at pictures * and * , talk together and suggest what you think is happening in them and how the group members might be feeling.

You have about a minute for this, so don't worry if I interrupt you. *(2 minutes for groups of three)*

Candidates *1 minute*
(2 minutes for groups of three): ....
Interlocutor: Thank you.

I'd like you to imagine that a magazine is planning a feature called Group Think, which will look at how people interact and behave in different group environments. These pictures will be used to accompany the article.

Talk together about how being in a group can change the way we behave, in relation to the pictures shown. Then suggest one other type of group situation that could be included in the feature.

You have about three minutes to talk about this *(4 minutes for groups of three)*.

Candidates: *3 minutes*
(4 minutes for groups of three): ....
Interlocutor: Thank you. (Can I have the booklet, please?) [Retrieve Part 2 booklet.]

A

Magazine Article – Group Behaviour

B

C

D

Speaking Section

Speaking Section

Interlocutor: Now, in this part of the test you're each going to talk on your own for about two minutes. You need to listen while your partner is speaking because you'll be asked to comment afterwards.

So (Candidate A), I'm going to give you a card with a question written on it and I'd like you to tell us what you think. There are also some ideas on the card for you to use if you like. All right? Here is your card.
Place Part 3 booklet, open at Task 1(a), in front of Candidate A.

Please let (Candidate B) see your card. Remember (Candidate A), you have about 2 minutes to talk before we join in.
[Allow up to 10 seconds before saying, if necessary: Would you like to begin now?]

Task 1(a):

> How can a country improve its Competitiveness to attract big companies to set up offices there?
> - workforce
> - tax
> - infrastructure

Candidate A (2 minutes): ....   **Interlocutor:** Thank you.

Interlocutor: *Ask one of the following questions to Candidate B:*
- Do you think your country has a highly-skilled workforce compared to others?
- Would you describe your country's infrastructure as ultra-modern?
- Why do governments want big international companies to set up offices in their countries?

> *Invite Candidate A to join in by selecting one of the following prompts:*
> - What do you think?
> - Do you agree?
> - How about you?

Candidates (1 minute): ....   **Interlocutor:** Thank you. (Can I have the booklet, please?) *Retrieve Part 3 booklet.*

Interlocutor: Now (Candidate B), it's your turn to be given a question. Here is your card.
Place Part 3 booklet, open at Task 1(b), in front of Candidate B.

Task 1(b):

> What are the benefits of competition in sport?
> - performance
> - spectacle
> - national pride

Please let (Candidate A) see your card. Remember (Candidate B), you have about two minutes to tell us what you think, and there are some ideas on the card for you to use if you like. All right?
[Allow up to 10 seconds before saying, if necessary: Would you like to begin now?]

Candidate B (2 minutes):   ....   **Interlocutor:** Thank you

Interlocutor: *Ask one of the following questions to Candidate A.*
- Why are countries often more competitive in some sports than others?
- Why does the general public become so absorbed by the performance of its national teams in sport?
- What makes some sports more popular with audiences than others?

> *Invite Candidate B to join in by selecting one of the following prompts:*
> - What do you think?
> - Do you agree?
> - How about you?

Candidates (1 minute): ....   **Interlocutor:** Thank you

Interlocutor: Now, to finish the test, we're going to talk about living arrangements in general.
(up to 4 minutes) Address a selection of the following questions to both candidates:

- Why are human beings so competitive in nature?
- What are the drawbacks of competition in sport?
- How does competition affect relationships between family members?
- How do customers benefit from high levels of competition amongst businesses?
- Is it necessary to have lost to truly appreciate winning?
- Should competition be encouraged at school from a young age?

Candidates (4 min):   ....   **Interlocutor:** Thank you. That is the end of the test.

TEST 8

Paper 4: SPEAKING
Time: 16 minutes per pair of candidates

Students take the Speaking test in pairs (occasionally, where there is an uneven number of candidates, three students may be required to take the test together). There are two examiners (an assessor and an interlocutor) and one of them (the assessor) does not take part in the interaction but assesses your performance according to four analytical scales. The other examiner (the interlocutor) conducts the test and tells you what you have to do. The interlocutor also gives you a global mark for your performance in the test as a whole.

Paper 4 Speaking   PART 1   (2 minutes / 3 minutes for groups of three)

In **Part 1** of the Speaking test, you may be asked to talk about your interests, general experiences, studies or career, and plans for the future. The examiner will first ask you for some general information about yourself, and then widen the scope of the conversation to include subjects like leisure activities, studies, travel, holiday experiences and daily life. Respond directly to the examiner's questions, avoid very short answers, and listen when your partner is speaking. You are not required to interact with your partner in this part, but you may do so if you wish.

Interlocutor: Good morning/afternoon/evening. My name is .... and this is my colleague .... And your names are .... ? Could I have your mark sheets, please?   Thank you.

First of all, we'd like to know something about you.
Where are you from (Candidate A)? And you (Candidate B)?
[address Candidate B] Are you working or studying at the moment?
[address Candidate A] And you?

Select a further question for each candidate:
- Are you on any social networks? (Do you use them much? What for?)
- How difficult would it be for you to have to live without Facebook and Twitter and so on?
- What, from your perspective, is the most beneficial aspect of having access to the internet?
- Are you more inclined to eat three large meals in a day, or do you like to snack often?
- Do you think your diet could be improved? (How?)
- What do you see yourself doing in 20-or-so years from now?

Candidates: ....
Interlocutor: Thank you.

Paper 4 Speaking   PART 2   (approximately 4 minutes / 6 minutes for groups of three)

Magazine Article – Speaking in public

Now, in this part of the test you're going to do something together. Here are some pictures showing a variety of different situations in which people are required to give speeches or talk in public.

Place Part 2 booklet, open at Task 1, in front of the candidates. Select two of the pictures for the candidates to look at.

First, I'd like you to look at pictures * and * and talk together about which situation you believe would be the more stressful.

You have about a minute for this, so don't worry if I interrupt you. *(2 minutes for groups of three)*

Candidates *1 minute*
(2 minutes for groups of three):   ....
Interlocutor: Thank you.

I'd like you to imagine that a magazine is planning a feature on speaking in public. These pictures will be used to accompany the article.

Talk together about the types of things people making speeches in public probably worry about, in relation to the pictures shown. Then suggest one other type of concern that could be represented in the images which accompany the magazine feature.

You have about three minutes to talk about this *(4 minutes for groups of three).*

Candidates: *3 minutes*
(4 minutes for groups of three):   ....
Interlocutor: Thank you. (Can I have the booklet, please?) [Retrieve Part 2 booklet.]

Speaking Section

Speaking in public

A

B

C

D

Paper 4 Speaking | **PART 3** | (approximately 10 minutes) | **Friendship**

Now, in this part of the test you're each going to talk on your own for about two minutes. You need to listen while your partner is speaking because you will be asked to comment afterwards.

So (Candidate A), I'm going to give you a card with a question written on it and I'd like you to tell us what you think. There are also some ideas on the card for you to use if you like. All right? Here is your card.
Place Part 3 booklet, open at Task 1(a), in front of Candidate A.

Please let (Candidate B) see your card. Remember (Candidate A), you have about 2 minutes to talk before we join.

Task 1(a):

> How do people become very close friends?
> * Shared experiences
> * Shared interests
> * Working together

Candidate A (2 minutes):   ....   **Interlocutor:** Thank you.

Interlocutor: *Ask one of the following questions to Candidate B:*
* Can any friend ever really be fully trusted?
* Why is friendship so important to us as human beings?
* What are the dangers of relying on just one or two close friends?

> *Invite Candidate A to join in by selecting one of the following prompts:*
> * What do you think?
> * Do you agree?
> * How about you?

Candidates (1 minute):   ....   **Interlocutor:** Thank you. (Can I have the booklet, please?) *Retrieve Part 3 booklet.*

Interlocutor: Now (Candidate B), it's your turn to be given a question. Here is your card.
Place Part 3 booklet, open at Task 1(b), in front of Candidate B.

Task 1(b):

> What sorts of things can cause a friendship to come to an end?
> * Moving home
> * Marriage and family issues
> * Breakdown in trust

Please let (Candidate A) see your card. Remember (Candidate B), you have about two minutes to tell us what you think, and there are some ideas on the card for you to use if you like. All right?
[Allow up to 10 seconds before saying, if necessary: Would you like to begin now?]

Candidate B (2 minutes):   ....   **Interlocutor:** Thank you

Interlocutor: *Ask one of the following questions to Candidate A.*
* Should family always come first – before friends I mean?
* In what ways can marriage and having children be tough on the husband and wife's own personal lives?
* Do you think it is possible to trust someone again if they have betrayed you? For example, if a wife cheated on her husband, or if your best friend revealed your biggest secrets to someone else.

> *Invite Candidate B to join in by selecting one of the following prompts:*
> * What do you think?
> * Do you agree?
> * How about you?

Candidates (1 minute): ....   **Interlocutor:**   Thank you

Interlocutor: Now, to finish the test, we're going to talk about success in general.
(up to 4 minutes) Address a selection of the following questions to both candidates:
* To what extent do you agree that all types of relationships have to be worked at?
* Why are some people more liked than others?
* Is popularity and having lots of friends a sign of a 'good' person?
* Is it quite normal now for people of different classes and cultures to become friends, or is it still rare?
* Why do an increasing number of people have large online networks of friends that they hardly ever see face-to-face?
* What sorts of health issues can those who become isolated face?

Candidates (4 min):   ....   **Interlocutor:** Thank you. That is the end of the test.

Additional Questions for Part 1

Part 1 *(2 minutes / 3 minutes for groups of three)*

Select one or more questions from any of the following categories, as appropriate.

Family and Friends
- How important do you think family is? …(Why?)
- How much time do you spend with your family and what do you enjoy doing with them?
- What qualities does a close friend need to possess?
- With whom would you discuss a difficult personal situation, a family member or a close friend? …(Why?)

Art
- What would you say is your relationship with the arts?
- Which kind of art are you most interested in? …(Why?)
- When was the last time you visited a museum, gallery or an exhibition? What were your impressions on this visit?
- Who is your favourite artist? …(Why?)

Sports
- Do you prefer team sports or individual sports?
- What qualities do you need to possess in order to do well in a team sport?
- What do you think about extreme sports?
- What are the most popular sports in your country?

Celebrities
- What are some of the advantages and disadvantages of being famous?
- Who is your favourite celebrity? …(Why?)
- What would you be willing to sacrifice in order to be famous?
- Why do you think more and more young people nowadays long for fame and money?

Education
- What is/was your favourite subject in school?
- What educational achievement are you most proud of?
- What is/was the most difficult subject for you in school? Why?
- Do/did you like or dislike school? Why or why not?

Local Area
- What is your favourite thing about your local area?
- What would you do to improve your local area?
- What is there to do around where you live?
- What is one reason people would like to move to your area?

Food
- What is your favourite food?
- What is your least favourite food?
- Tell me about a restaurant you like to eat at.
- What foreign foods have you tried?

Future Plans
- What are your goals over the next few years?
- Where do you see yourself in ten years?
- What skills would you like to gain in the future?
- Tell me something about your future plans regarding work.

Recent Experiences
- What is something exciting you've done in the past year?
- What is something new you've tried recently?
- What have you done this past year?
- Have you accomplished anything special recently?

Additional Questions for Part 1

Part 1 *(2 minutes / 3 minutes for groups of three)*

Select one or more questions from any of the following categories, as appropriate.

The Environment
- What problems are there concerning the environment in the area that you live in?
- In your neighbourhood, is recycling a part of people's everyday life?
- Pollution is a very serious issue in our days. In what way(s) are you trying to protect the environment?
- Are you a member of any environmental group? Have you ever considered being one?

Leisure Time
- What do you like to do in your free time?
- Are you an active individual? In what ways?
- Creativity in life is very important. In what ways do you usually express yourself?
- Is there enough free time for you to refill your energy for your routine days?

Lifestyle
- What food do you like? Are you a vegetarian or a meat eater?
- Are you practising any sport? Any connection between your diet and a sport philosophy (i.e. yoga)?
- Smoking is a dangerous habit, though many people smoke without considering the hazards to their health.

Health
- Do you think you have a healthy lifestyle? Why or why not?
- What do you do for exercise?
- Do you think a vegetarian diet is healthy or not?
- Do you think people should be allowed to smoke in restaurants? In bars?

Culture
- Describe one thing that is important in your culture.
- Do you prefer to listen to music from your own country or from other countries?
- Do you think art should be taught in schools?
- Would you like to be an actor? Why or why not?

The Media
- Do you like keeping up with current events?
- Where do you get your news about the world?
- What do you think about advertisements on TV?
- How much influence do you think the media has
- on your life?

Speaking Section

Test 1

Reading

PART 1   Reading | **Questions 1-8**

For questions 1-8, read the text below and decide which answer (A, B, C or D) best fits each gap. Mark your answers on the separate answer sheet. There is an example at the beginning (0).

Example   **0 A** had   **B** even   **C** been   **D** done

| 0 | A | B | C | D |

The Invention of Television

Few inventions have (0) *had* more scorn and praise (1).......... them at the same time than television. And few have done so much to unite the world into one vast audience for news, sport, information and entertainment. Television must be (2).......... alongside printing as one of the most significant inventions of all time in the (3).......... of communications. In just a few decades it has reached (4).......... every home in the developed world and an ever-increasing proportion of homes in developing countries. It took over half a century from the first suggestion that television might be possible before the first (5).......... pictures were produced in laboratories in Britain and America.

In 1926 John Logie Baird's genius for publicity brought television to the (6).......... of a British audience. It has since (7).......... such heights of success and taken on such a pivotal function that it is difficult to imagine a world (8)............ of this groundbreaking invention.

1.	A	taken over	B	heaped upon	C	picked on	D given over
2.	A	awarded	B	rated	C	graduated	D assembled
3.	A	location	B	site	C	post	D field
4.	A	simultaneously	B	actually	C	virtually	D substantially
5.	A	flaring	B	glimmering	C	sparkling	D flickering
6.	A	attention	B	concentration	C	initiation	D surveillance
7.	A	found	B	left	C	gained	D reached
8.	A	without	B	shallow	C	bereft	D lacking

PART 2   Reading   Questions 9-16

For questions 9-16 read the text below and think of the word which best fits each gap. Use only one word in each space. There is an example at the beginning (0).

Example: **0**   **LIKE**

The Subconscious and the Human Mind

The human mind is **(0)** *like* an onion with many layers. The outer layer is our conscious mind, which helps with our daily decision-making processes working **(9)**..................................... to the reality principle. It is intelligent, realistic, logical and proactive, **(10)**..................................... in new situations where we have to employ rational thought processes to **(11)**..................................... out what to do and how to do it. However, it can only deal with **(12)**..................................... five and nine things at any one time and is easily overloaded.

The subconscious or main hidden layer of the onion works **(13)**............................ "auto pilot" i.e. reacting according to the pleasure principle in **(14)**............................ it seeks to avoid pain and obtain pleasure and survival, **(15)**........................ of external considerations. It is concerned with our emotions, imagination, and memories as well as our autonomic nervous system, which controls our internal organs automatically. **(16)**..................................... four main functions are very closely interlinked; in other words, the mind affects. It is powerful and very clever at dealing with many complex instructions simultaneously, but is not 'intelligent' as such.

PART 3   Reading   Questions 17-24

For questions 17-24, read the text below. Use the word given in capitals at the end of the lines to form a word that fits in the space in the same line. There is an example at the beginning (0).
Write your answers **IN CAPITAL LETTERS** on the separate answer sheet.

Example: **0**   *international*

Battle to Save the Amazon

As the Brazilian **(0)** *international* plane banked over the Amazonian rainforest, **(17)**.....................................	NATION
Ghilean Prance gazed at the dark-green canopy below: an expanse of trees almost **(18)**.....................................	BOTANY
for 2.5 million square miles, with more **(19)**..................................... of plant and animal life than any other place	BREAK
on earth.	VARY
Few **(20)**..................................... knew more about the rainforest and its ecosystem than Prance. He had just	OUT
been appointed **(21)**..................................... of postgraduate studies at the National Amazonian Research Institute	DIRECT
in Manaus, the Amazonian region's capital. Before that, as research assistant at and latterly a curator of the	
(22)..................................... New York Botanical Garden, he had spent almost ten years studying the forest.	PRESTIGE
In his search for new plant specimens he was more used to travelling on foot or by boat. But now,	
Brazilian **(23)**..................................... documents show that a road had been constructed through the Amazon	GOVERN
basin. On this bright November morning he was flying out with two other course tutors and 14 botany	
(24)........................ to make sure its impact on the surrounding habitat was not as serious as he thought.	STUDY

PART 4 Reading | **Questions 25-30**

For questions 25-30, complete the second sentence so that it has a similar meaning to the first sentence, using the word given. Do not change the word given. You must use between three and eight words, including the word given. Here is an example (0).

Example:

0   Mick will give you lots of excuses for being late but don't believe any of them.

matter

No .... Mick gives you for being late, don't believe any of them.

Write only the missing words on the separate answer sheet.

0	matter how many excuses

---

25. His argument was irrelevant to the case being discussed.

nothing

His argument .... the case being discussed.

26. Karen sometimes appears very silly.

apt

Karen .... very silly sometimes.

27. His aggressive attitude shocked me.

aback

I .... his aggressive attitude.

28. I did my best to arrive here on time.

effort

I .... get here on time.

29. The meal was delicious apart from the chicken.

exception

.... , the meal was delicious.

30. The match had to be cancelled due to the bad weather.

called

The match .... of the bad weather.

You are going to read an extract from an article. For questions 31-36, choose the answer (A, B, C or D) which you think fits best according to the text. Mark your answers on the separate answer sheet.

Taming the Wildcat

Now, I have had, at one time or another, a fair amount of experience in trying to get frightened, irritated or just plain stupid animals to feed from a bottle, and I thought that I knew most of the tricks. The wildcat kitten I had, proceeded to show me that, as far as it was concerned, I was a mere tyro at the game. It was so lithe, quick and strong for its size that after half an hour struggling, I felt a total failure. I was covered in milk and blood and thoroughly exhausted, whereas the kitten regarded me with blazing eyes and seemed quite ready to continue the fight for the next few days if necessary. The thing that really irritated me was that the kitten had – as I knew to my cost – very well developed teeth, and there seemed no reason why it should not eat and drink of its own accord, but, in this stubborn mood, I knew that it was capable of quite literally starving itself to death.

I decided to try another tack. Perhaps it would eat if I had a companion to show it how. I chose a fat, placid female tabby cat and carried it back to the garage. Now most wild animals have a very strong sense of territory. In the wild state, they have their own particular bit of forest or grassland which they consider 'their' preserve, and which they will defend against any other member of their own species that tries to encroach. When you put wild animals into cages, cages become, as far as they are concerned, their territory, too. So if you introduce another animal into the cage, the first inmate will, in all probability, defend it vigorously, and you may easily have a fight to the death on your hands. So you generally have to employ low cunning. Suppose, for example, you have a large spirited creature and you get a second animal of the same species, and you want to confine them together. The best thing to do is build an entirely new cage, and into this you introduce the weaker of the two animals. When it has settled down, you then put the stronger one in as well. The stronger one will, of course, still remain the dominant animal, but as far as it is concerned it has been introduced into someone else's territory, and this takes the edge off any potential viciousness.

In this case I was sure that the baby wildcat was quite capable of killing the domestic kitten, if I introduced the kitten to it instead of the other way round. So, once the tabby had settled down, I seized the wildcat and pushed it, snarling and raving, into the cage, and stood back to see what would happen. The tabby was delighted. It came forward to the angry intruder and started to rub itself against its neck, purring loudly. The wildcat, taken aback by this greeting, merely spat rudely and retreated to a corner. I covered the front of the cage with a piece of sacking and left them to settle down.

That evening, when I lifted the sacking, I found them side by side, and the wildcat, instead of spitting at me as it had done up until now, contented itself with merely lifting its lips in a warning manner. I carefully inserted a large bowl of milk into the cage, and a plate of finely chopped meat and raw egg, which I wanted the wildcat to eat. This was the crucial test.   *line 60*

The tabby, purring like an ancient outboard engine, flung itself at the bowl of milk, took a long drink then settled down to the meat and egg. To begin with, the wildcat took no interest at all, lying there with half-closed eyes. But eventually the noise the tabby was making over the meat and egg – it was rather a messy feeder – attracted its attention. It rose cautiously and approached the plate, as I watched with bated breath. Delicately it sniffed around the edge of the plate, while the tabby lifted a face that was dripping with raw egg and gave a mew of encouragement, slightly muffled by the portion of meat it had in its mouth. The wildcat stood pondering for a moment and then, to my delight, sank down by the plate and started to eat. In spite of the fact that it must have been extremely hungry, it ate daintily, lapping a little raw egg, and then picking up a morsel of meat, which it chewed thoroughly before swallowing. I knew my battle with the wildcat was won.

31. **How did the wildcat make the writer feel?**

    A. anxious

    B. inadequate

    C. cunning

    D. stubborn

32. **The wildcat**

    A. was injured.

    B. couldn't eat because it had problems with its teeth.

    C. was dying of starvation.

    D. was capable of starving but wasn't yet in a state of starvation.

33. **Why did the writer put the tabby cat in the cage first?**

    A. to make it aggressive.

    B. the stronger animal will still remain dominant

    C. to give it a chance to eat

    D. to make it the dominant animal

34. **How did the wildcat originally react to the tabby?**

    A. it welcomed it

    B. it attacked it viciously

    C. it made contented noises

    D. it rejected it

35. **Why was the test "crucial" in line 60?**

    A. Because the tabby might have prevented the wildcat from eating.

    B. The wildcat might have attacked the tabby.

    C. It was the moment that would determine the outcome of the attempt.

    D. The wildcat might have attacked the writer.

36. **What can be assumed from the fact that the wildcat ate "daintily"?**

    A. It wasn't as hungry as the writer had thought.

    B. It didn't like the food.

    C. It felt at ease.

    D. It felt self-conscious

You are going to read an article about media coverage of the weather. Seven paragraphs have been removed from the extract. Choose from the paragraphs A-H the one which fits each gap (37-43). There is one extra paragraph you do not need to use. Mark your answers on the separate answer sheet.

Getting up early on the morning of January 24th, I thought the city seemed oddly quiet, but it wasn't until I looked out the window that I saw the snow. The "Surprise Storm" that had hit the East Coast of the United States that morning was making earnest headway, having dumped as much as twenty inches of snow on Raleigh, eight and a half on Philadelphia, and six on New York. This was a big shock considering the unusually mild weather that had been settled over New York as recently as just a day ago.

37

Forecasters had seen a low-pressure system moving toward the southeast on the National Weather Service's satellite pictures, but all the major computer models indicated the storm would head back out to sea. As Elliot Abrams, the chief forecaster and senior vice-president of the State College, Pennsylvania, forecasting company Accu-Weather, told me later, "Who am I to say the numerical guidance is wrong?"

38

Ever since widespread weather-data collection began, shortly after the invention of the telegraph, in the 1840s, accurate forecasting has been the goal of the weather report. But in recent years TV weather has given increasing time and emphasis to live pictures of weather, usually in the viewing area, but sometimes elsewhere if the weather is atrocious and the pictures dramatic enough – and this is transforming the modern-day weather report.

39

The Weather Channel acknowledged this in a recent ad created by Chiat/Day which depicted weather enthusiasts in the guise of sports fanatics, their faces painted like weather maps, rooting for lows and highs in a fictional "weather bar" known as the *Front*. At the same time, the news, which once stuck to human affairs, now includes an ever-growing number of weather-related stories.

40

And the weather's upward climb in the newsworthiness stakes has also coincided with another trend; wild weather is also now a standard component of reality-based programming on Fox and the Discovery Channel. And in book publishing recent best-sellers like "*The Perfect Storm*", "*Into Thin Air*", and "*Isaac's Storm*" have helped create a hot market for weather-related disaster stories.

41

This newsier approach to weather, with its focus on weather events to help boost ratings, means certain kinds of weather get overblown while less telegenic but no less significant weather is overlooked. Take heat, for example. Eight out of the ten warmest years on record occurred in the nineteen-nineties, the two others in the eighties. (If the planet continues to warm at the present rate, some climatologists predict an increase in global surface temperatures of between 2.5 and 6 degrees by the year 2100.)

42

This is an old complaint - that ratings-driven, storm-of-the-century-style coverage makes it harder to get accurate information about the weather - and it has been heard here in New York at least as far back as when the over-hyped Hurricane Gloria struck in 1985.

43

However grateful we may be for this lack of danger, through war and bloodshed, it creates a psychological need for some kind of real-life drama on our TV screens. So, when a big storm comes along, you can almost feel the nation girding its loins as people gratefully turn their attention away from "Who Wants to be a Millionaire?"

A

But heat doesn't do particularly well on television. You can track down a blizzard on Doppler radar as it moves up a map of the East coast, but you can't watch heat. And drought, as Robert Henson, a writer at the University Corporation for Atmospheric Research and the author of a book about TV weather-casting, told me recently, "is the ultimate non-event. You usually hear about drought only when some rain event comes along to end it."

B

From 1989 to 1995, according to the Centre for Media and Public Affairs, weather coverage wasn't among the top-ten topics on the nightly network news. In 1996, it was eighth, and in 1998 it was fourth – more than eleven hundred weather-related stories ran together.

C

For the previous three weeks, unreasonably balmy conditions had been the topic of small talk everywhere: Why was it so warm? Wasn't it weird that there was no snow? Was it another sign of global warming? Then, wouldn't you know, the first big storm of the season comes along, and the National Weather Service, the federal government's agency, doesn't put out an advisory until ten o'clock the night before. (The N.W.S. had been on the network news just a week earlier, announcing new weather super computers, which are supposed to make forecasts even more accurate.)

D

Opinions concerning the causes of global warming remain highly contentious. But many climatologists now believe that rising temperatures produce more extreme weather - not just more frequent heatwaves and droughts but also more storms and floods.

E

But it's not only the broadcaster's doing: the public's fascination with wild weather is apparently inexhaustible. We live in peaceful, prosperous times, when the only tangible external threat to home and hearth is weather.

F

This is not so much a new market, though, as a revival of one of the oldest genres in publishing. This increased in Mather's 1684 book "*Remarkable Providences*", which includes several chapters on extreme weather around New England and was one of the early thrillers of the New World.

G

In some respects, these broadcasts seem more like news than like "weather" in the traditional sense. Weather "events" are hyped, covered, and analyzed, just like politics and sports.

H

I turned on the Weather Channel, as I always do for big storms. The forecast may have been inadequate, but the live coverage was superb. In New York City, the Weather Channel was out in force, filming cars driving through slushy puddles and reporters sticking rulers into the snow in Central Park. I settled in for a little voyeuristic weather-watching, an experience that has become a condition of modern life.

You are going to read an extract from an article on two books. For questions 44-53, choose from the sections (A-E). The sections may be chosen more than once.

Mark your answers on the separate answer sheet.

In which section are the following mentioned?

the feeling of being responsible for a death	**44**
the problem of putting literature into categories	**45**
another novel referred to in the novel	**46**
using language in different ways	**47**
characters who don't easily accept change	**48**
the refusal to embrace the way of life of either of two elders	**49**
different types of colonies	**50**
one of the novels being made into a film	**51**
death playing a role to help a community	**52**
the difficulty in defining the sub-genre of certain publications	**53**

A

Both *Purple Hibiscus* and *Once Were Warriors* are post-colonial novels, in the sense that they were written, and deal with subjects of the position of independence as opposed to the colonial state of being in both a universalising sense and a personal one. *Purple Hibiscus* was published in 2004 and is set in Nigeria, the author Cinamanada Ngozi Adichie's homeland. *Once Were Warriors* was written by a Maori New Zealander, Alan Duff, in 1990 and has since met with international acclaim through the silver screen. But, what has contributed to making this is another lengthy tale. Both books sit happily on the shelf labelled "postcolonial literature," but such careless sweeps of the categorising tongue are exactly what such authors are attempting to avoid. Their works don't reinforce the boundaries, leaving readers feeling warm and cosy. Colonialism, precolonialism and a whole set of other blunt "isms" can be argued as being explored by these authors.

B

That remnants of colonialism and pre-colonialism are present in each text indicates the boundaries between pre-colonial and colonial states of being are not as established, in a post-colonial existence, as the frame of the words denote. What are the implications of depicting, potential pre-colonial situations within the colonial tongue? Both *Once Were Warriors* and *Purple Hibiscus*, potentially present colonial and pre-colonial notions of history or histories, but from different post-colonial positions. With Nigeria having been a colony of occupation, as opposed to the settler colony of New Zealand, relations between the coloniser and the colonised differ greatly between the two cultural entities. With the coloniser, potentially, obscuring and abstracting the area between pre-colonial and postcolonial existences, any pre-colonial notions must always be partly located within a colonial perspective. Nonetheless, the precolonial uttered in the colonial tongue renders that colonial tongue as being somewhat altered in the process. The colonial tongue both makes and unmakes itself by using the same tools for different ends. The dragging of heels back and forth over the hot coals of second-hand languages renders the happy branding of "postcolonial" of those who dare to make the colonial tongue their own seem like an unrefined broad-brushes attempt to depict the hairline cracks in a china doll.

C

Both texts deal with the uncertainties of the formation and reformation of identities. Working with, yet at the same time questioning and unsettling, the bildungsroman format, *Once Were Warriors* and *Purple Hibiscus* present identities snaking through notions of pre-colonial identities alongside colonial and postcolonial ones. The certainty of the very survival of Kambili and Beth in *Once Were Warriors* seems, to an extent, to be staked on pre-colonial notions of identity formation. The chief at Beth's funeral articulates this in sorrow for the young girls death; 'we are what we are only because of our past [...] we should never forget our past or our future is lost'. The death of Grace directly influences Beth to address her situation and that of the individuals in Pine Block. Although Grace's death is linked to the rape, Beth, who is unaware of this, questions her involvement in the death of her daughter. 'Could I have prevented it?' echoes out from every movement Beth makes after this. Why does the young girl have to die? Is it to highlight injustices in the Maori community, to make the community, to an extent, stand up and demand to be heard?

D

Indeed, it is death that stalks the corridors of these two novels. It is the death of Eugene, the 'colonial product' in *Purple Hibiscus* alongside the death of Papa-Nnukwu the 'pre-colonial product' that lead to questions of where to turn in terms of identity formation. The colonial figure is dead; he doesn't present ways of being to his children that seem acceptable to them; he is too violent, too dominating for their generation. But, as well, Papa-Nnukwu, who is adored by his grandchildren, seems like an inadequate role model to wholly guide the younger generation into futures that are still in the making.

E

By introducing *Purple Hibiscus* with the sentence 'Things fall apart', Adichie is immediately paying homage to Chinua Achebe's same-named novel published in the mid-twentieth century, which depicted a hamlet in Africa on the eve of nineteenth-century colonialism. Everyday lives and everyday disputes fill page after page. The reader is with the hamlet when its inhabitants are devastated. We are invited to sit in another seat. To see how it might have felt to be utterly subjugated by foreigners. The beauty of comparing the two Nigerian novels is in their dealings with Christianity. Indeed, in *Things Fall Apart*, church missionaries come to the hamlet to 'save them from hell and damnation' and Okonkwo, the head of the hamlet, is immediately distrustful. He is closed to change as is the Catholic 'colonial product' of Eugene in *Purple Hibiscus*. The stubbornness each character shows, but towards different ends, demonstrates the meaninglessness of assertions of power for the sake of assertions of power.

PART 1   Writing   **Question 1**

Read the two texts below.

Write an essay summarising and evaluating the key points from both texts. Use your own words throughout as far as possible, and include your own ideas in your answers.

Write your answer in **240-280** words.

1.

Organic Shopping

Organic food sales have rocketed in the past decade, but how many of those who buy organic food understand what GM (Genetically Modified) food actually is? A hundred years ago, in some parts of the world everything was organic; therefore, nothing was organic. It has also come to represent something of privilege nowadays in that those able to pay for it tend to be financially better off. Not buying organic food can even cause raised eyebrows in certain circles almost like the openly-GM shopper is a sinner.

Organic food: the way to a healthier and happier future

Organic farming was developed in reaction to the use of large-scale farms and the introduction of chemicals into farming practices. A large number of people don't want to feed chemically-drenched apples to themselves or their families. The side effects of consuming these chemicals aren't entirely known yet, but vast numbers of people are simply unwilling to take the risk. Not only are these chemicals potentially harmful to humans, but also to the habitats on which they are sprayed.

Write your **essay**.

PART 2 Writing   Questions 2-4

Write an answer to **one** of the questions **2-4** in this part. Write your answer in **280-320** words in an appropriate style on the separate answer sheet. Put the question number in the box at the top of the answer sheet.

2. A local magazine has asked readers to send in articles on their preferences in public transport. Say which methods you prefer, explain your reasons and assess whether or not your preferences are similar to those of the majority of people where you live. If there are problems with some forms of transport say what they are and what might be done about these problems.

   Write your **article**.

3. You have been playing a historically based game as part of an afterschool club. You have agreed to write a review about the game for the club's website. In your review you should give your opinion of the game and say whether you think games are a good way of learning about history.

   Write your **review**.

4. An online blog in English has invited readers and visitors to send in emails sharing embarrassing things that have happened to them. You decide to send an email to them in which you briefly describe an embarrassing story. Say whether you think these embarrassing moments help us and explain why.

   Write your **email**.

Listening

You will hear three different extracts. For questions 1-6, choose the answer (A, B, or C) which fits best according to what you hear. There are two questions for each extract.

EXTRACT 1

You will hear a woman describing her feelings as she observes people at an airport.

1. While waiting for her plane, the speaker
   A. is nervous about the journey ahead.
   B. feels sad because there is no one to see her off.
   C. has mental pictures of her family.

2. The speaker
   A. feels comforted by her experiences of travelling.
   B. becomes upset by the memory of her grandfather's death.
   C. becomes nostalgic about her husband.

EXTRACT 2

You hear an interview with one of the oldest people in the world.

3. Jeanne
   A. has many elderly relatives.
   B. puts her longevity down to genetics.
   C. plays a lot of sport.

4. Jeanne likes to
   A. go out with nurses in the home.
   B. make others take part in charity events.
   C. keep herself occupied.

EXTRACT 3

You hear information for parents about children and drug abuse.

5. Children
   A. are naturally curious about drugs.
   B. are bound to take drugs at some time.
   C. need to be threatened in order to stop them from taking drugs.

6. Every parent
   A. should encourage their children to try safe drugs.
   B. should censor what their child reads or watches on TV.
   C. should listen to their child's ideas about drugs.

You will hear a radio report about Mensun Bound, a world-famous marine archaeologist.
For questions 7-15 complete the sentences with a word or short phrase.

Martha Ballard reports that

Mensun dives to explore [7 _____] in the ocean.

Mensun is the [8 _____] of a TV programme.

Mensun's travel onwards from Patagonia took him on a [9 _____].

The Metropolitan Museum of Art awarded him a(n) [10 _____].

Mensun's undergraduate study in New York was [11 _____].

Mensun has been a marine archaeologist for [12 _____].

Some wreck divers just want to make money from [13 _____].

Mensun believes the archaeological finds provide a lot of [14 _____]

for people.

Mensun wishes he could accept every [15 _____] that he

receives.

PART 3 Listening **Questions 16-20**

You will hear an interview with Kip Keino, a Kenyan Olympic athlete. For questions 16-20, choose the answer (A, B, C or D) which first best according to what you hear.

16 African runners
   A. have won all the middle distance competitions recently.
   B. have learned a lot from successful British runners.
   C. have dominated some running events over the last 25 years.
   D. beat the British world record holders in Athens.

17 The farm
   A. brings in substantial profits.
   B. acts as an orphanage.
   C. is in the town of Eldoret.
   D. has stopped him from running for a living.

18 Kip seems to be
   A. nervous
   B. pessimistic
   C. grateful
   D. compassionate

19 The children
   A. are encouraged to leave the farm when they finish school.
   B. often have a difficult time at the farm.
   C. are expected to get a good job.
   D. are free to do as they like after high school.

20 The farm is
   A. developing a new project.
   B. going to be transformed into a school.
   C. going to be totally funded by donors in the future.
   D. funded mainly by the church.

PART 4 Listening **Questions 21-30**

You will hear five short extracts with different people talking about adventure holidays.
You will hear the recording twice. While you listen, you must complete both tasks.

TASK ONE
For questions 21 – 25, choose from the list (A – H) what each speaker did on their adventure holiday.

A helped to build a school
B stayed in places for free
C stayed in a hotel
D stayed in accommodation that was built using traditional methods
E stayed in a canal boat
F stayed in a hard-to-reach part of a country
G shared a room with others
H got up early every morning

Speaker 1	21
Speaker 2	22
Speaker 3	23
Speaker 4	24
Speaker 5	25

TASK TWO
For questions 26 – 30, choose from the list (A – H) which benefit of going on an adventure holiday each speaker mentions.

A being away from the busyness of everyday life
B taking photographs
C being able to make decisions
D meeting different people
E being close to so many different species
F feeling healthy
G a chance to give something at the same time as enjoying oneself
H discovering new ways of doing things

Speaker 1	26
Speaker 2	27
Speaker 3	28
Speaker 4	29
Speaker 5	30

Test 2

Reading

| PART 1 Reading | **Questions 1-8** |

For questions 1-8, read the text below and decide which answer (A, B, C or D) best fits each gap. Mark your answers on the separate answer sheet. There is an example at the beginning (0).

Example   **0 A** that   **B** which   **C** discover   **D** wrote | **0** | **A** | **B** | **C** | **D** |

Pregnancy – a time to forget

Anecdotal reports (0) *that* heavily-pregnant women are more (1).......... have been (2).......... up by a study that has found that the ability to memorise information drops significantly in the last three months of pregnancy.

The findings of the study were reported yesterday to the Society for Neuroscience annual meeting in New Orleans by Dr Pamela Keenan, assistant professor of psychiatry at Wayne State University and Dedroit Medical Centre.

In a study into the "benign encephalopathy of pregnancy", Dr Keenan (3).......... memory tests on 19 pregnant women and found that the ability to (4).......... information declined during pregnancy. Expressed in (5).......... of the amount of information that could be remembered, it declined from 49 percent in the first trimester, to 47 percent in the second, to 39 percent in the third. Shortly, after birth the study participants were able to recall 52 percent of the information.

It was noted that after a period of approximately three months, the studied revealed that new mums' memories return to a relative (6).......... of normality. Other studies have since been carried out on more subjects revealing more (7).......... evidence that pregnancy does indeed contribute to memory-loss. But, then again, there are also health (8).......... to life with a bun in the oven.

1.	A resentful	B memorable	C forgetful	D oblivious
2.	A backed	B suppressed	C assumed	D persevered
3.	A carried over	B carried away	C carried on	D carried out
4.	A restore	B acknowledge	C allocate	D recall
5.	A times	B terms	C conditions	D references
6.	A state	B way	C behaviour	D situation
7.	A heavy	B understandable	C concrete	D weighed
8.	A advantages	B aid	C paths	D benefits

PART 2   Reading | **Questions 9-16**

For questions 9-16 read the text below and think of the word which best fits each space. Use only one word in each space. There is an example at the beginning (0).

Example: | 0 | CENTURY |

Early Calendars

Dennis the Small, a 6th (0) *century* expert on canon law, has had an enduring, if unsung, (9)............................... on the affairs of the modern world. It was (10)............................... to his calculations that the precise timing of the 2000th anniversary of Christ's birth was recently confirmed beyond (11)............................... . Dionysus Exiguus, as he was then (12)............................... , was charged in 525 by Pope John I with setting dates in the Christian calendar. Though he was a good mathematician, the accuracy of Dennis' calculations was limited by the information (13)............................... at the time.

Establishing the exact (14)............................... of Christ's crucifixion — and therefore that of Easter — (15)............................... an especially difficult challenge. Theologians had decreed that Easter should be marked on the Sunday after the first full (16)............................... after the vernal equinox, but without accurate solar and lunar calendars how could the church fathers predict the dates in the future?

PART 3   Reading | **Questions 17-24**

For questions 17-24, read the text below. Use the word given in capitals at the end of the text to form a word that fits the space

Example: | 0 | difference |

A Trip Back in Time

Let's do the time warp and head back to 1973. What is the biggest (0) *difference*, you notice between life now and 40 years ago? Probably nothing more startling than the men's (17)............................... bouffant hairstyles.

In terms of the (18)............................... and pleasure offered by (19)............................... of the time, 1973 would provide a soft landing for Millennium Man. A trip back to 1973 would certainly not be a return to the Dark Ages. That said, in some ways, of course, 1973 does seem like a world away. In that year computer pioneers like Apple's (20)............................... , Steve Jobs, were still working out of garages and were entirely (21)............................... to the public; DVD was a meaningless combination of letters, with (22)............................... home video recording not set to appear for another two years.

One of the less (23)............................... developments in 1973 was ABS — one of the earliest consumer (24)............................... of computer micro-processors, which the Intel company in the States — long before it became a household name — had developed in 1970.

DIFFER
RIDICULE

CONVENIENT
/TECHNICAL

FOUND
KNOW
PRACTICE
SPECTACLE
APPLY

PART 4   Reading | **Questions 25-30**

For questions 25-30, complete the second sentence so that it has a similar meaning to the first sentence, using the word given. Do not change the word given. You must use between three and eight words, including the word given. Here is an example (0).

Example:

0   Mick will give you lots of excuses for being late but don't believe any of them.

   matter

   No .... Mick gives you for being late, don't believe any of them.

Write only the missing words on the separate answer sheet. | 0 | matter how many excuses |

25. It's impossible to say how he will react to your news.

   telling

   There .... react to your news.

26. He looks very similar to his brother.

   bears

   He .... to his brother.

27. You are not the only person to fail this exam.

   alone

   You .... this exam.

28. We can't promise that we'll be back in time.

   guarantee

   There .... we'll be back in time.

29. He was really jealous when he saw his brother's new car.

   green

   He was .... see his brother's new car.

30. This new bar is much better than the old one.

   improvement

   This new bar .... the old one.

You are going to read an article concerning the role of literature as an art form. For questions 31-36, choose the answer (A, B, C or D) which you think fits best according to the text. Mark your answers on the separate answer sheet.

Making a Living

It is my opinion that literature is at the same time and at once the most intimate and the most articulate of all the art forms. It is impossible for it to impart its effect through the senses or the nerves as can other forms of art; it is beautiful only through the intelligence of both the reader and writer; it is the mind speaking to the mind; until it has been put into absolute terms, of an invariable significance, it does not exist at all. It is able to awaken one emotion in one person and a totally different emotion in another; if it fails to convey precisely the meaning of the author, if it isn't an expression of him or her, it says nothing, and thus it is nothing. So that when a poet has put their heart and soul, more or less, into a poem, and has sold it to a magazine, the scandal is far greater than when a painter has sold a picture to a paying patron, or a sculptor has modelled a statue to order, or a photographer has produced a landscape photograph for a popular magazine. These are artists less articulate and less intimate than the scribe; they are more removed from the work they produce; they are often less personally involved in their work; they part with less of themselves.

That Tennyson, Longfellow and Emerson sold their poems and essays – works in which they had couched the most mystical messages their genius was charged to bequeath to mankind – does not, however, diminish the virtuosity of their achievements. They submitted to the conditions which no one can escape, which are nonetheless the conditions of hucksters because they are generally imposed upon poets and writers. If it will serve to make my meaning clearer, we will suppose that a poet has been crossed in love, or has suffered some bad fortune or some real sorrow, like the loss of a wife or child. He pours out his broken heart in verse that shall bring tears of scared sympathy from his readers, and an editor pays him a hundred pounds for the right of bringing his verse to their notice and for allowing them to print it in their publica-

tions. It is perfectly true that the real reason that the poem was written was not for the monetary benefit, but it is also perfectly true that it was sold for it. The poet is forced into using his emotions to pay his bills; he has no other means of making a living; society does not propose to pay his bills, for him, after all, so what choice does he really have? Yet, at the end of the day, the unsophisticated witness finds the transaction ridiculous, repulsive, and, to a great extent, exploitative. Yet deep down they are perfectly aware that if our huckster civilisation did not at every moment violate the relationships we undertake in the world, the poet's song wouldn't have been given to it, and the scribe wouldn't have been extolled by the whole of humanity, as any human should be who does the duty that every human owes it.

The instinctive sense of the dishonour which money brings to art is so strong that sometimes men and women of letters able to pay their bills, to pay their way through others means, refuse money for their work, as Lord Byron did, from a noble conscience. But Byron's publisher profited from a generosity which did not reach his readers; and the Countess Tolstoy collects the copyright royalties which her husband forgoes; so that these two instances of protest against business in literature may hardly be said to have shaken the world of commerce in literature to the core of its money basis. I know of no others but there may be many that exist of whom I am culpably ignorant. Still, I would very much doubt if there are enough to affect the fact that literature has become business as well as art. At present, business is the only human solidarity; we are all bound together with that chain, whatever the interests, tastes and principles that otherwise separate us.

31. **The author implies that writers**

A. are not sufficiently paid for their work.

B. are incompetent in business.

C. profit against their will.

D. are greedy.

32. **What does the author lament about Tennyson, Longfellow and Emerson?**

A. They wrote mystical poems.

B. They had to sell their poetry and essays.

C. They were not appreciated in their time.

D. They were prolific poets.

33. **What does the author propose that writers and artists should do?**

A. Make the best of a bad situation.

B. Attempt to induce society to change its values.

C. Withhold their work until they gain recognition.

D. Produce purely commercial, rather than original work.

34. **What does the author say about creators accepting payment for their works of literature or art?**

A. The works of art can be justified in terms of society's wants and desires.

B. They are part of the degeneration of the human condition.

C. They are writing and painting solely for monetary gain.

D. They share their life experiences with society.

35. **According to the author what did Lord Byron do?**

A. He didn't financially gain from his literary pursuits.

B. He combined literature with business.

C. He copyrighted his work to help his wife.

D. He became well-known in the business community.

36. **The writer of the article seems to suggest that**

A. writing literature is a good way to get rich quickly.

B. the integrity of works of literature is not greatly undermined by their commercialism.

C. literature is appreciated by businessmen and professionals generally.

D. literature causes divisions amongst people.

PART 6   Reading   Questions 37-43

You are going to read an extract from an article. Seven paragraphs have been removed from the extract. Choose from the paragraphs A-H the one which fits each gap (37-43). There is one extra paragraph you do not need to use. Mark your answers on the separate answer sheet.

For the world's population, access to an injection-programme and general good health shouldn't be a matter of the luck of the draw. Scientific advances have concentrated on diseases more prevalent in richer countries and appear to have neglected the plight of the poor - especially in third world countries - suffering from diseases that are routinely classified as easily preventable.

37

The good news is that we can save these lives. Measles, polio, whooping cough, yellow fever – diseases that debilitate, disfigure and kill millions of children can be prevented with existing vaccines. Parents in developing countries often walk miles, or pay high prices to get the shots. They know that their children need some vaccines that parents in developed countries take for granted.

38

When we first turned our attention to philanthropy, it seemed natural to extend technology to classrooms and libraries. Technology clearly can transform and empower its users. But our thinking crystallised as we learned of an even greater need – impoverished children stricken with preventable diseases. One man has already made a great difference in the world.

39

The power of vaccines – the most cost-effective medical intervention ever invented – lies in their ability to prevent rather than treat disease. It's often the case that it is not until we become parents that we fully appreciate the virtues of having a form of medical intervention that protects before limbs go limp or hearts stop beating. Today vaccines save the lives of some 3 million children each year – children who are fortunate enough to have been born in countries with effective health systems, adequate vaccination supplies and trained health personnel.

40

Access to safe, effective vaccines to such diseases should not be dictated by circumstance. That is why a commitment was made by the Global Fund for Children's Vaccines a year ago. The goal of the Global Fund, and the partners of the Global Alliance for Vaccines and Immunisation, is to ensure that every child has access to lifesaving vaccines. An estimated 6 billion pounds over the next five years will cover the cost of fully immunising children in developing countries.

41

In the 1970s only 5% of the world's children could expect to be fully immunised. Today, thanks to these "rich" nations, alongside the work of countless dedicated health professionals worldwide, we can envision a time when 70, 80, and finally 100 percent of children are protected. And at a cost of 10 to 15 pounds per child, vaccines are a small investment for a very big return.

42

The dedication of resources to speed the discovery of new vaccines must also be a priority. Scientists and organisations like the International AIDs Vaccination Initiative are currently working to develop vaccines for the top three killer diseases – AIDs, Malaria, and tuberculosis. If they find them, perhaps the more daunting challenge will be to distribute them to those who need them most.

43

Ghandi once said that for him the Golden Rule meant that he could not enjoy things denied to other people. We should strive to ensure that health and freedom from these terrible diseases is something that no parent is denied.

A

A. But even the greatest of parental effort can't help if the vaccines aren't available. In the past it has taken up to 15 years for newly developed vaccines – including the relatively recent hepatitis B vaccine – to become available in poor countries. Those delays are measured in childhood fatalities. Our challenge is to provide every child, regardless of where they live or their family's economic status with access to lifesaving vaccines.

B

There has also been a concerted effort by governments and other organisations to raise sufficient funds to save children's lives through immunisation. Some governments should be applauded for their active support and substantial donations to the cause.

C

The new philanthropy blends 1960s social consciousness with the present financial model. SO far donations have topped eight and a half million pounds to help inoculate children in India against the three major killer childhood diseases.

D

Dr. Jonas Salk changed the world when he announced the discovery of the polio vaccine. His work started a vaccine revolution, and, as a result, millions of children have escaped the disease's crippling and often fatal effects. The last reported case of wild polio in the Western Hemisphere was in 1991. Who would have dreamt back in 1953 that within a generation – our generation – we would see polio almost eradicated from the face of the earth?

E

Vaccines cannot work their magic without a global effort. Parents, world leaders, and foundations can and should work together because we all want the same thing for our children, and this is something that great, humanitarian leaders have been aware of for a very long time.

F

Whether they live in Bangladesh, Botswana or Seattle, all parents want the best for their children. Providing a healthy start in life and through childhood is a priority for every family. Yet for all the amazing advances we have made so far in medicine, there are still far too many children who don't have access to even the most basic healthcare. More than 2 million die each year from vaccine-preventable diseases. This is a staggering statistic – a tragic reality we have ignored for too long. It is global news when an airline crashes, but rarely newsworthy that 228 children die from preventable illnesses every hour of every day. It's time to move this issue of immunisation to the top of our global agenda.

G

But there is more to do. First we need to redouble our efforts to introduce newer vaccines more quickly. It is heart-wrenching and unacceptable that children in the developing world may have to wait a decade or more to receive vaccines that are already saving lives in richer countries.

H

Yet tens of millions of people do not share in these benefits because of what they can afford or where they live. World-wide, more than 1 billion people live on less than 50p a day. Lack of safe water, poor sanitation and meagre food supplies are part of the grim reality of their daily lives. Their children weakened by malnutrition, and parasitic infections, are susceptible to childhood killers – whooping cough, measles and meningitis.

PART 7 Reading | **Questions 44-53**

You are going to read an extract from a book on the railway in India. For questions 44-53, choose from the sections (A-E). The sections may be chosen more than once. Mark your answers on the separate answer sheet.

In which section is the following mentioned?

an important Indian figure using the railway station for a meeting about the nation   **44** ☐

the cutting up of land   **45** ☐

two countries doing the same thing with their railway networks at the same time   **46** ☐

violence in relation to the railway   **47** ☐

the using of Indian workers to build railways in other countries   **48** ☐

a totally new nation of the time   **49** ☐

the railway playing a part in violence   **50** ☐

the railway as a place on which to write messages   **51** ☐

a physical feature of the currency of India   **52** ☐

the railway wasn't built to be used as a tool for creating a nation   **53** ☐

Nationing India through the Railway

A　Within Raja Rao's Kanthapura, the railway is present in its supporting interactions between the village and the city, and the Congress Party and their village supporters, in delivering newspapers and directions of actions to take in the anti-imperial and nationalist movement. Notions of the railway delivering messages of anti-colonial sentiment can be found in it presenting a surface which is translatable as a canvas in nationalistic graffiti. As Kurt Iveson suggests, in relation to the railway in Australia, 'if the train' that carries graffiti 'runs' with the tag [or message] still on it, this gives the writer [or a movement] more recognition.' So, the railway can be seen to open the possibility of literally carrying intentions towards nationhood on its very surface. The railway, of course, was not built by the British with intentions towards independence, but can be seen to introduce a particular framework that comes to be appropriated in the movements towards nationhood.

B　Not only can the railway be seen as a mobiliser of nationhood, but conterminously as a mobiliser of capitalism. As Ian Kerr suggests in *Building the Railways of the Raj*, the building of the railway in India introduced the framework of contractual employment - of the labour market - and, the knowledge of the saleability of that labour, arguably, lays the foundations for unions, The Congress Party and ultimately independence. Independence and the conceiving of the nation internationally can be further perceived in the participation of Indian construction workers in the building of railways throughout Africa. The knowledge of the saleability of labour internationally anticipates the falling of borders through globalisation before their construction. As Barrack Obama arrives at the old Nairobi train station in the post aspect of colonialism, he writes upon a railway line that had taken 'the lives of several hundred imported Indian workers' for the 'line of track that helped usher in Kenya's colonial history', inferring an interconnectivity within the Empire, and an interconnectivity within the constructing of railways and, furthermore, how that 'colonial history' relied upon the introduction of the railway.

C　In Deepa Mehta's film, Water Chuyia is a child-widow, in an institution for women whose husbands have died. After living in this institution and witnessing the curtailing of happiness and freedom, she is taken to the railway station. Gandhi is reported to have been released from prison and is rumoured to be holding one of his 'prayer meetings' in the station. As Chuyia is carried to the station, the procession of people heading towards Gandhi has a slowness and a reverence similar to pilgrims entering a temple in anticipation of witnessing a god. Indeed, in post-colonial India, Gandhi's face is printed on the national currency of India, and he is referred to as the 'father of the nation.' The holding of a politico-religious meeting in the railway station further supports the proposition that the railway played a key role in nation building and independence. The final shot of the train proceeding into the future carrying the child-widow, Narayan the Gandhiist, and Gandhi himself invokes a positivist sense of 'inevitability' of 'progression' and nationhood.

D　The scene set in the railway station in Deepa Mehta's *Earth* focuses upon Ice Candy Man crouching on a platform at Lahore railway station amongst others waiting for the train to arrive from the recently split Punjab, and the newly partitioned India. In breaking away from the British, the land and the railway is being reclaimed and rewritten upon; the process of cracking is entered into, revealing gaps and lapses in time and memory. As the train arrives twelve hours late, an uncanny silence draws up next to it; a silence that is echoed with the arrival of the 'ghost train' of Khushwant Singh's Train to Pakistan. In *Earth*, those waiting for the arrival of the train expect to meet family members and the one-day-old citizens of the newly formed nation of Pakistan; instead, the unnervingly silent carriages divulge death and dis-memberment. The communicative aspect of the railway network becomes traumatically fulfilled; the railway carries the conflicting messages of renewal and relief, and bloodshed and war. The men are described as having been butchered and the women as having been dismembered with the 'members' filling gunny sacks. The witnessing of divided bodies echoes the land that has itself had incisions made upon it.

E　Arriving in India in 1947, the train indeed shows its availability to both the colony and the nation. With its origins lying beyond the border of independence, and with its route having taken a course through the violent bordering in partition, the railway can be seen to have participated in narratives that have also been plastered on it tracks. In this, the railway network, once again, comes to inhabit a position of ambivalence; it balances precariously upon colonial narratives, partition narratives and post-colonial narratives without retaining a secure position in any. It is in this ambivalence that one can read the railway as analogous to the nation. If the railway network can be seen as contributing to movements towards nationhood, and, perhaps, even directly supporting nationhood, then the nationalising of the railway after the Second World War in both India and Britain demonstrates how important the railway was regarded in relation to the nation and, indeed, to power at that time.

Writing

PART 1   Writing   **Question 1**

Read the two texts below.

Write an essay summarising and evaluating the key points from both texts. Use your own words throughout as far as possible, and include your own ideas in your answers.

Write your answer in **240-280** words.

1.

> ### *Fairtrade or not fair trade*
>
> With so many products now bearing the logo "fairtrade" and with those companies still seeming to make huge profits, it's difficult to believe that they are giving all they can. It is also the case that "fairtrade" has become a brand name that needs to promote itself for the sake of its own survival rather than the farmers it is meant to be supporting. The "fairtrade" association can only retain the public's respect if it is the boss of companies joining the bandwagon not the other way round.

> ### *Fairtrade is the only hope for some farmers*
>
> The success the "fairtrade" association is seeing of late is causing some to raise their eyebrows. It's strange that when an organisation is little-known yet fighting hard, people like it, but when this little-known organisation begins to realise some of its goals, those same supporters turn away. It's true the "fairtrade" association hasn't achieved what it set out to, but it has not by a long shot given up. Those who are losing respect for the association because of its sudden success need to rethink who they are really turning their backs on: the poor farmers producing chocolate and coffee for a pittance.

Write your **essay**.

Write an answer to **one** of the questions **2-4** in this part. Write your answer in **280-320** words in an appropriate style on the separate answer sheet. Put the question number in the box at the top of the answer sheet.

2. The library in your town or college is going to be expanded. Write a letter to the Planning Committee explain how you think the present facilities could be improved and suggest some new services that the library could provide better.

    Write your **letter**.

3. You have just completed a one-week practical training course paid for by your employers. Write the report required by your employers, describing the course content and its usefulness, and saying whether you would recommend it for other members of staff.

    Write your **report**.

4. You are a member of a group which is seeking to improve the quality of life for elderly people in your neighbourhood. Write an article for the local newspaper explaining the aims of your group, how people can join it, and what they can do to help.

    Write your **article**.

Listening

PART 1   Listening   Questions 1-6

You will hear three different extracts. For questions 1-6, choose the answer (A, B, or C) which fits best according to what you hear. There are two questions for each extract.

EXTRACT 1

You hear a psychologist talking about drama.

1. According to new research
   A. it's hard to tell if we are awake or dreaming sometimes.
   B. dreams usually tell us what we really want from life.
   C. dreams illustrate what is happening in our life.

2. How are women's dreams different to men's?
   A. Women never dream about strangers.
   B. Women usually know the people in their dreams.
   C. Women become very emotional after a dream.

EXTRACT 2

You hear a radio presenter talking to a doctor.

3. Body Dysmorphic Disorder
   A. affects most people at some time in their life.
   B. prevents people seeing themselves realistically.
   C. affects people who are unattractive.

4. Sufferers of BDD
   A. are usually cured by having cosmetic surgery.
   B. are always bullied at school.
   C. don't always believe that only one part of their body is ugly.

EXTRACT 3

You will hear a sociologist talking about how one can improve one's social skills.

5. In order to keep a conversation going you should
   A. pay attention to the person speaking to you.
   B. not appear too relaxed.
   C. look the person in the eyes until they look away.

6. Which ot the following shouldn't you do?
   A. Talk about your children too much.
   B. Ask personal questions.
   C. Give oral prompts to show you are listening.

PART 2 Listening **Questions 7-15**

You will hear a radio report about how to develop your brain.
For questions 7-15 complete the sentences with a word or short phrase.

Martin Clark reports that

There are about **7** [_____] neurons in the brain.

Our thoughts cause tiny **8** [_____] to travel to the brain.

Phrenologists of the 19th century believed different parts of the brain controlled one's
9 [_____] .

The connections made between neurons is compared to somebody's
10 [_____] .

We **11** [_____] by not using our entire brain.

The creative part of the brain is in the **12** [_____] section.

The right back part of our brain controls **13** [_____] .

The four areas of the brain are compared to **14** [_____] that need to be used.

The left back part of your brain is essential for people who need to exercise
15 [_____] in their work.

PART 3   Listening   Questions 16-20

You will hear an interview with a hypnotist. For questions 16-20, choose the answer (A, B, C or D) which first best according to what you hear.

16   The interviewer believes that
A. hypnosis is a specialized form of entertainment.
B. hypnosis as a form of entertainment can't be justified.
C. some entertainers don't use hypnosis in a morally correct manner.
D. it is unethical to use hypnosis as a form of entertainment.

17   One of the things about hypnosis is that it
A. allows people to concentrate on one aspect of their life.
B. encourages people to be more analytical.
C. can only work if you are already deeply relaxed.
D. will help you to sleep deeply after a session.

18   In order to be hypnotised
A. you need to get written consent.
B. you must be sober.
C. you'll probably have to try many different methods.
D. you may feel as if you are drunk.

19   Hypnotherapy
A. is not recommended for people with addictions.
B. can be used to change a person's habits.
C. is a therapist's most powerful tool
D. gives you more control over the way people perceive you.

20   During a session,
A. people often forget what was said.
B. people regularly come out of the trance prematurely.
C. people usually fall asleep for a short amount of time.
D. people sometimes resist coming out of a trance.

PART 4   Listening   Questions 21-30

You will hear five short extracts with different people talking about reading.
You will hear the recording twice. While you listen, you must complete both tasks.

TASK ONE
For questions 21-25, choose from the list (A-H) what each speaker is speaking about.

A plays
B research journals
C novels
D encyclopaedias
E poetry
F magazines
G instruction booklets
H newspapers

Speaker 1	21
Speaker 2	22
Speaker 3	23
Speaker 4	24
Speaker 5	25

TASK TWO
For questions 26-30, choose from the list (A-H) which main purpose reading serves for each speaker.

A to inform for a specific reason
B to learn about different countries
C to find out about gossip
D as a last resort
E to appreciate the often overlooked details in the world
F to escape from reality
G to broaden the mind
H to relax

Speaker 1	26
Speaker 2	27
Speaker 3	28
Speaker 4	29
Speaker 5	30

Test 3

Reading

PART 1   Reading | **Questions 1-8**

For questions 1-8, read the text below and decide which answer (A, B, C or D) best fits each gap. Mark your answers on the separate answer sheet. There is an example at the beginning (0).

Example   **0 A** all   **B** everything   **C** one   **D** nothing

The sinking of the Titanic

All in (0) *all* the Titanic had received six ice warnings; it was quite clear that the Titanic was steaming towards ice. At 11.40 pm many of the stewards were turning down the lights and cleaning the Titanic's public rooms and the last of the social (1).......... were now breaking up. Meanwhile in the crow's nest, Frederick Fleet and Reginald Lee struggled to (2).......... what was in the haze - for some (3).......... reason binoculars were not in the nest. Suddenly Fleet jerked the warning bell three times and telephoned the bridge and sputtered, "Iceberg dead (4).......... .!" into the receiver. "Thank you", Sixth Officer Moody replied. The Titanic was on a collision (5).......... with a huge iceberg and the officers in the crow's nest (6).......... themselves for impact. The worst part is what happened to the people onboard. The ship was one of the most luxurious liners of all time, but it wasn't (7).......... with enough lifeboats for the passengers, so many died that night and in the (8).......... hours of the following morning.

1.	A	gatherings	B	conferences	C	summits	D	congregations
2.	A	see off	B	look ahead	C	keep out	D	make out
3.	A	A. insecure	B	eccentric	C	alien	D	odd
4.	A	A. before	B	ahead	C	beyond	D	forward
5.	A	A. crash	B	way	C	course	D	track
6.	A	A. rehearsed	B	anticipated	C	braced	D	nurtured
7.	A	A. built	B	fitted	C	carried	D	floated
8.	A	A. young	B	low	C	early	D	starting

CPE Practice Test 3

PART 2 Reading | **Questions 9-16**

For questions 9-16 read the text below and think of the word which best fits each space. Use only one word in each space. There is an example at the beginning (0).

Example: **0**   COMES

"Winter in Madrid"

When winter **(0)** ....*comes*...., I hurry to Madrid. I love the noisy, cosy winter bars and the restaurants where diners tuck

(9)......................... garlic soup.

No **(10)**......................... it is a case of early imprinting – I lived and worked in Madrid when I was younger, teaching as so

(11)......................... of us do. Later, as a visiting journalist, I **(12)**......................... a tiny role in chronicling the demise

(13)......................... the Franco dictatorship. And always, I loved the winter the best. Today, I nurture the belief that others

will find it as exciting as I do when most of the tourists, save **(14)**......................... the odd straggler, have gone home.

I **(15)**......................... to say it can rain in winter in Madrid – sometimes quite **(16)**......................... – but the sun usually makes

an appearance again within a matter of hours; the sky bright blue, as in a landscape by the Flemish master Joachim Patinir.

PART 3 Reading | **Questions 17-24**

For questions 17-24, read the text below. Use the word given in capitals at the end of the lines to form a word that fits in the space in the same line. There is an example at the beginning (0).

Example: **0**   **recognition**

What will we do for work?

I believe that 90% of white-collar jobs in the US will be altered; beyond **(0)** _recognition_ in the	RECOGNISE
next 10-15 years. That's a catastrophic **(17)**......................... given that 90% of us are engaged in	PREDICT
white-collar work. Even most manufacturing employees these days are connected to white-collar	
(18)......................... .	SERVE
In 1970 it took 108 men about five days to **(19)**......................... the timber from one ship.	LOAD
Then came containerization. The **(20)**......................... task today takes eight men one day.	COMPARE
That is a 95.5% **(21)**......................... in man-days.	REDUCE
Nowadays, new technology **(22)**......................... companies to accept and easily	ABLE
(23)......................... projects which would, in the past, have presented major headaches	TAKE
in order to bring them to **(24)**......................... .	FRUIT

PART 4 Reading | Questions 25-30

For questions 25-30, complete the second sentence so that it has a similar meaning to the first sentence, using the word given. Do not change the word given. You must use between three and eight words, including the word given. Here is an example (0).

Example:

0   Mick will give you lots of excuses for being late but don't believe any of them.

     matter

     No .... Mick gives you for being late, don't believe any of them.

Write only the missing words on the separate answer sheet. | **0** | matter how many excuses |

25. She is proud of being so fit.

    prides

    She .... so fit.

26. I phone her nearly every day.

    goes

    Hardly .... her.

27. I never intended to give him the job.

    no

    I .... him the job.

28. If you don't work harder, you'll fail the exam.

    socks

    You .... if you want to pass the exam.

29. I feel totally relaxed after a nice warm bath.

    leaves

    A nice warm bath .... totally relaxed.

30. I'm quite happy to go on holiday alone.

    averse

    I'm .... on holiday on my own.

You are going to read a psychological report about survival at sea. For questions 31-36, choose the answer (A, B, C or D) which you think fits best according to the text. Mark your answers on the separate answer sheet.

Survival at Sea

What happens psychologically when one is lost at sea? Why does one person survive while another perishes? Is there a personality type that makes one person better at handling the elements, fear and loneliness? Until recently, science has been completely in the dark about what makes a survivor. Now experts are intensifying their search to demystify the psychology of survival, analysing personality traits among people who triumph over life-threatening crises – and those who succumb.

In a life-threatening situation the brain immediately triggers a state of shock, sending alarms through the body. Your emergency response system shifts into gear. Blood pressure rises, muscles tense, adrenalin pumps. If you survive initially, you then shift mental gears to longer-term planning – whatever you have to do to survive. Next you go into the resistance phase; a chronic coping state, in which the body tries to maintain balance in the face of threat, danger and deprivation.

Later, one of two things happens: you enter an exhaustion phase, in which the coping mechanisms are overwhelmed, you lose strength, and die – as often happens – or you persevere long enough and get rescued or escape the situation. Who survives, it turns out, isn't determined by age, physical stamina, or experience. Although one would expect people who are fitter to be the best candidates to make it back alive, the mind, that great trickster, isn't ruled by logic.

Last summer, for example, a sailboat sank. It was being sailed by Nicholas Abbott, who often transported pleasure boats from the Caribbean to New York. With him was his friend, Janet Culver, a reserved woman, not a risk-taker, making her first long-distance cruise. If you worked for an insurance agency, you'd bet Abbott would be the one to return alive. Yet he's the one who died. After 10 days adrift in a tiny dinghy, battling 16-foot waves and thundershowers, Abbott – hungry, thirsty, and delirious – said he was going to swim home, jumped overboard and drowned. Culver, covered with sun blisters and too weak to sit, would not give up. "Each day I stayed alive was another chance to be res-

cued", she told me. "Something deep inside told me to hang on one more day." While Abbott let his depression get the better of him, Culver evaluated her situation in small, manageable increments. She kept her mind open. It is important to remain mentally active, dwelling on positive things. "Don't give up", say the experts. "Dive your thoughts to things that make you happy. Have fantasies." In other words, play games with your mind. Don't let it play tricks on you, which experts say it does.

The mind goes from hope for rescue, to isolation, to depression. These feelings come, go and vary in order. You have a better chance of survival with other people there. Just being able to say "I'm not going to do what he's doing" helps handle negative thinking. Highly destructive is the "last chance" phenomenon: rescue is visible, but they don't see you. You start thinking "that was my only chance; they won't be back again!" Then you feel doomed. In the end, long-term exposure causes delirium. You start drinking salt water, which causes more delusions. In the cold, people sometimes start shedding garments and a trail of clothes is found. Paradoxically, these people interpret their coldness as warmth.

Researchers studying people who triumph over life-threatening crises are finding survivors share common personality traits: high self-esteem and optimism. Often the difference in mental, rather than physical toughness determines who will endure. Survivors often have a strong belief system outside themselves, in family and religion. Once you give into the sense of abandonment, you give up. Survivors tend to be tenacious in a self-preserving way. They do the right things under pressure. Even though Culver was technically less skilled at sea, she didn't lose her head. Abbott panicked, left the safest position, and exposed himself to death. The experts attribute this fighting spirit to an immeasurable factor. They can measure weight, age, sex, swimming ability, flotation, quality of clothing – finite things. But they can't measure the will to live. The only true measure of it is who stares into the abyss and doesn't blink.

31. **Until recently, scientists**

    A. had no knowledge of why some people are less vulnerable.

    B. had been experimenting with people in extreme situations.

    C. believed that the personality of a survivor was defined by fear.

    D. had not been interested in what makes a survivor.

32. **According to the writer,**

    A. the exhaustion phase is preceded by a failure of coping mechanisms.

    B. survival depends on how healthy you are.

    C. you need to be intelligent to survive a dangerous situation.

    D. there are a number of phases in the survival process.

33. **Why is it surprising that Janet Culver survived?**

    A. She had never been sailing before.

    B. She didn't take Abbott's advice.

    C. She didn't appear to have a very strong character.

    D. She was nervous of being at sea.

34. **What is one reason why the presence of other people with you in a survival situation can sometimes help you to survive?**

    A. They tell you not to give up.

    B. You can play games with them to keep awake.

    C. They can remind you of how not to behave.

    D. They can help you look out for rescue vehicles.

35. **Why is near-rescue destructive?**

    A. It makes the person lose hope.

    B. The person knows they will not get another chance.

    C. It causes delirium.

    D. People usually try to swim to the rescue vessel.

36. **Why can't scientists measure the will to live?**

    A. Because it is different in every person.

    B. Because it is an abstract quality.

    C. Because it changes throughout a person's life.

    D. Because people are reluctant to be analysed in such a way.

PART 6   Reading   Questions 37-43

You are going to read an extract from an article. Seven paragraphs have been removed from the extract. Choose from the paragraphs A-H the one which fits each gap (37-43). There is one extra paragraph you do not need to use. Mark your answers on the separate answer sheet.

A drive through a phobia

Motorways are the safest roads in Britain. I read that somewhere not long ago – and a fat lot of good it's done me. For I am slowly surrendering to a terror of motorway driving. Just a glimpse of the sign that warns "Motorway Traffic Only" and I feel as if I am about to fall off the edge of the Earth.

37

I will even convince myself that this makes more sense – that, really, the route through a strange town in rush hour is quicker, that there is bound to be a hold-up on the more obvious routes.

38

Until recently, the open road never used to be a problem. I have driven across America and back. I have driven across Malaysia. I have been a night-time minicab driver, speeding across London and the Home Counties in the hours before dawn. I have even negotiated North America's Long Island Expressway in hot summer rush hours. But now I cannot get myself onto the M25.

39

My GP was the obvious starting point, but the procedure involves a referral, a wait of weeks, possibly months, and then a month or two of weekly visits to a clinical psychologist. A friend suggested driving lessons might do the trick.

40

But that's nothing to do with the phobia – which left two or more esoteric American treatments to sample. First, I visited Frank Gerryts in Twickenham, west London, who uses the new "emotional freedom technique". "EFT is to do with releasing energy blocks", said Gerryts. "A phobia is a learnt response. At some stage, you have to learn to be scared of whatever it is. You learn quickly and remember forever. But you can also unlearn it."

41

"Your phobia is like a forest: each tree is an aspect of it," said Gerryts. "If you focus in on a tree and cut it down, eventually, you've cleared a space. Cut down enough of those trees and suddenly they aren't a problem." And that's all there is to it. It's quick, easy – and supporters claim a near-100% success rate. It would be marvellous: except, in my case, it did no good at all.

42

NLP started in the late 1970s in America. "It is outcome-orientated", said Bean. "It will give you a clear idea of what you want and help you achieve it. NLP can help us become who we want to be." I wanted to be a person who drives on motorways.

Bean made me imagine I was sitting in a cinema seat. Then I left my body in the seat and took my mind to the projectionist's booth, from where I watched a film of myself driving on a motorway, in colour and in black and white, forward and backward. After that, I felt I could handle Spaghetti Junction in a wet, dark rush hour. Sadly, when faced with the M40 in drizzle, I decided to leave it for another day. I did not really want to go to Banbury anyway.

43

As a life disrupter, a fear of driving on motorways doesn't come close to a fear of buttons or police officers. And driving phobias, says Blowers, are relatively simple to treat. So, once I have overcome my phobia about paying him 90 pounds an hour, for up to 10 sessions of 90 minutes or so, he's the man for me. Until then, I can always take a train. After all, it's better for the environment.

A

Next I tried the NLP (neurolinguistic programming) phobic cure. This, said Gary Bean, whom I visited in Teddington, southwest London, is "fast, so straightforward it can be taken up by anyone – and 100% successful."

B

These are all classic signs of a phobia: a usually irrational fear or hatred of some sort. My terror of the M-word certainly does not seem rational, even to me – you are three times as likely to get killed on an A-road, despite nearly 9,000 motorway crashes involving injury each year. Brampton wrote about her fear of driving in Vogue magazine. What a revelation! I tentatively mentioned.

C

This fear crept up slowly so I hardly noticed it happen. Then, a few months ago, a friend of mine, Sally, said the same thing had happened to her, and, suddenly, felt like everyone had the same problem – or knew somebody who did. So, like one in 10 of the population, I had a phobia. Nobody knows for sure how or why they start, but once I had acknowledged my condition, I was ready to go in search of a cure.

D

I suppose some people have a fear of driving abroad. That is a more logical phobia as one is unfamiliar with a foreign country. I personally have never tried driving abroad, but as long as it wasn't on a motorway, I suppose I'd cope.

E

Eventually, I rang the Priory, refuge of the confused, depressed and addicted, in Putney, London. Colin Blowers, a behavioural therapist, offered words of comfort and a "reasonably high success rate" through gradual exposure, starting by just sitting in a car or even, in severe cases, standing near one. Eventually he will follow people as they drive onto a motorway, or talk them through it by mobile phone.

F

The thought of trying to join that relentless stream of thundering traffic gives me the creeps – thumping heart, cold shivers, sweaty palms. My hands actually slip on the wheel before I bottle out at the last second, turning with relief back to the nice, safe A-road, with all its comforting delays and frustrations.

G

Bryan Lynn, the chief examiner of the Institute of Advanced Motorists, agreed, "People who aren't used to motorway driving can be a little intimidated by the speed and the volume of the traffic", he said. "They need to go out with someone who understands, to ease them through it." But this doesn't explain why it suddenly develops. I asked what sort of person is typically frightened of six-lane highways. "Ladies in later middle age", came the horrible reply. "Hubby has unfortunately passed away, and hubby has always driven the car."

H

Together, we chose an aspect of my fear (getting on the slip road) and then, while rubbing a spot on my chest, I had to repeat the following three times: "Even though I have this fear of slip roads, I deeply and completely accept myself." This concentrates the mind. Then you have to tap your face and your collarbone while repeating the bit about the slip road. If any emotional intensity remains, you repeat the whole lot before picking another aspect of the problem.

PART 7   Reading | **Questions 44-53**

You are going to read an extract from an article on gender. For questions 44-53, choose from the sections (A-E). The sections may be chosen more than once.

Mark your answers on the separate answer sheet.

In which section are the following mentioned?

the details of a linguist's theory   44 [   ]

Judith Butler's ideas around the distinction often made between gender and sex   45 [   ]

the disagreeing of a philosopher with a linguist's theory   46 [   ]

the possibility of using Judith Butler's work to improve a situation   47 [   ]

sexism towards women by members of the same sex   48 [   ]

the misinterpretation of a term in Judith Butler's work   49 [   ]

the worst problems of gender-assignment   50 [   ]

the difficulty in trying to summarize Judith Butler's ideas   51 [   ]

the surrounding of human beings in language   52 [   ]

that people today aren't that different from people of a different era   53 [   ]

Neither this nor that

A Most of us sit happily within our binary categorised genders. We push the boundaries a little bit. We like to think we're being a bit alternative with our decisions in clothing, or even in attitude. It isn't difficult to find perfectly straight househusbands taking an interest in the decor of the family home and to find misogynistic women in boardrooms and on factory floors alike across the globe today. We might be able to do more within our assigned gender, but we're still very much pinned down by the borders of our gender – we're still only reacting against our strict Victorian predecessors – we've yet to step into the future of our possible selves.

B A difficult pill for us to swallow though is that we can't imagine ourselves without gender. Who are we without our box labels of "man" and "woman". As we ask ourselves this question, a beautiful songbird flies past our eyes and it dawns on us that we don't exist without these categories. Or, rather we cannot imagine – we are unintelligible to ourselves without these demarcations. This is one of the basic ideas of Judith Butler, a theorist on many aspects of identity, but who made her name in the public domain with her research upon gender. She works from within a number of perspectives and any cursory attempt at an introduction to her and her ideas would be to do unto her a great injustice, but for those who are unfamiliar with her work, she argues that gender is performative. This term has, indeed, caused some of the many problems and confusions with Butler's theory, but as a base from which to start, one who would like to understand should soon dispose of the theatrical notion hanging around in your connotational mind and turn towards the field of linguistics. More specifically towards a particular linguist and his work; J. L Austin's *How To Do Things With Words*.

C J. L. Austin's work couldn't be further away from gender studies if it tried, but Judith Butler made use of his famous theory upon the performativity of certain types of speech or utterances. He argued that some utterance had no reference outside of the sentence, so these utterances are performative. Austin refers to the utterances in naming ceremonies and marriage ceremonies as instances of the performativity of language. It takes a while to get one's head around this, but essentially Austin argues that in certain cases utterances do not describe nor state the "doing" of an action, but rather the utterance itself is the action; the utterance performs the action. "I name this ship..." would be an example of a performative utterance. Judith Butler arrives at Austin's work through a critique of it by the French philosopher Jacque Derrida. Derrida takes issue with Austin's narrow usage of his theory.

D This is where Judith Butler picks up the thread. She argues that from the moment we are born, we are encased by language. We don't speak back for a year or so, but the people around us are already dressing us up in the finery of the language we will one day use to decorate ourselves – to create our identities with. But, further than this and more explicitly as Butler develops in her later work *Bodies That Matter*, the moment we are born the sentence is uttered "it's a girl" or "it's a boy" – this is the basis of her argument of gender being performative. I suppose a good way to imagine it is through Spiderman's web that he shoots from his wrist. The web is language and language that is inescapable. The implications of this though, are very serious for Butler. She often writes about children who are born with two sets of genitals or whose genitals are ambiguous. For these people, Butler argues, the "gendering" is most cruel. These human beings aren't left as the beautiful products that they are, but quite the opposite – they are mutilated as babies and find it very difficult to live sexually fulfilling lives as adults.

E Although never explicitly stated in Judith Butler's work, what her work might lead onto is the lessening of the gendering process. She would be incredibly sceptical about such an idea. She would suggest that this was impossible; that we cannot think outside of the gendered categories. She believes that the only way to make life more bearable in the gendering process is through subversion. One way she suggests is to overdo gender. She argues that the hyperbolically feminine and the hyperbolically masculine draw attention to the edges of the categories whilst at the same time undermining the categories by the very fact of their borders. Some would suggest you see, that man and woman, male and female (Butler has a very interesting perspective when it comes to the pop-science differentiation between "gender" and "sex" with the latter often being read as "biological" and the former as "cultural") are related to the notion of "nature". The househusband who takes an interest in the decor of the family home would probably complacently suggest that, in nature, women would usually do this and men would do that, but because we live in a society that allows for the reverse, we can do otherwise. Butler would have problems with this for a number of reasons including the unquestioning usage of the term "nature".

Writing

PART 1   Writing   **Question 1**

Read the two texts below.

Write an essay summarising and evaluating the key points from both texts. Use your own words throughout as far as possible, and include your own ideas in your answers.

Write your answer in **240-280** words.

1.

Lock them up!

There is only one way to treat people who have committed a crime and that's to lock them up. All crimes deprive the victim of something – either of their life, of their possessions, or their power to say no, so when somebody decides to commit a crime, they should also have something taken away – their freedom. It is the only way to set a good example to children and teenagers – make sure they know that they will face heavy punishment for harming others.

Prison: the University of Crime

Sending people to prison doesn't necessarily help to prevent future crime. People who get sent to prison usually just come out as better criminals. Petty crime should not be punished as heavily as harder offences. If you send somebody to prison for stealing a phone, then they will spend time with people in prison who have committed much more serious crimes and, in the end, become influenced by them. The stealing of the phone might have been a desperate act, but if you send the perpetrator to prison, he may choose to become a professional criminal on being released.

Write your **essay**.

PART 2 Writing	Questions 2-4

Write an answer to **one** of the questions **2-4** in this part. Write your answer in **280-320** words in an appropriate style on the separate answer sheet. Put the question number in the box at the top of the answer sheet.

2. Your town is looking to use government money in a more efficient way. Write a letter to the mayor of your town to make suggestions of ways in which money could be saved.

    Write your **letter**.

3. Your language school is looking for better ways for students to learn. They don't have much money in which to buy high-tech equiprnent, but they would like to make any improvements that would be both cost-effective and learner-friendly. Write a report on ways in which to improve the school taking into account that it only has a relatively tight budget.

    Write your **report**.

4. You use an online resource for your studies. You would like people to take advantage of such resources, so you decide to write an article for your local newspaper. Write an article for the local newspaper describing the resource and explaining why you think it is useful.

    Write your **article**.

Listening

You will hear three different extracts. For questions 1-6, choose the answer (A, B, or C) which fits best according to what you hear. There are two questions for each extract.

EXTRACT 1

You hear an artist being interviewed.

1. What happened to the artist?
   A. His sculpture was never put in the place that he'd designed it for.
   B. A piece of his work was destroyed..
   C. A woman bought one of his sculptures illegally.

2. Why was the artist angry?
   A. No one consulted him about the removal of the sculpture.
   B. He wasn't paid enough money for the sculpture.
   C. Because artists are generally treated badly in Wales.

EXTRACT 2

You hear some information about theatres in London.

3. If you want a cheap theatre ticket
   A. it's a good idea to go to Leicester Square.
   B. you must be a student.
   C. you can only go to a matinee performance.

4. If you have a friend who uses a wheelchair you can
   A. get useful information at the British Travel Centre.
   B. go on a special theatreland tour for the disabled.
   C. only gain access to a few of the theatres.

EXTRACT 3

You will hear an artist being interviewed about his life.

5. How did his years in a concentration camp affect him?
   A. He became very angry and bitter.
   B. It made him famous enough to be knighted.
   C. He feels it was a positive influence.

6. According to Terry Frost
   A. he had no idea what his work was really about.
   B. you need to have an open mind while creating something.
   C. it's important to always remain optimistic.

PART 2 Listening   **Questions 7-15**

You will hear a radio report about the Getty Museum in Los Angeles.
For questions 7-15 complete the sentences with a word or short phrase.

Ruth Adams reports that

The Getty Museum looks like a(n)   **7** [   ]   stranded on land.

Another name for the San Diego Freeway is the   **8** [   ] .

The only way to get to the museum is by   **9** [   ] .

The six buildings of the museum are of great interest to   **10** [   ] .

It took   **11** [   ]   to design and construct the museum.

Only   **12** [   ]   parties are allowed before 11 am.

The museum has a fine collection of examples of 15th to 19th century   **13** [   ] .

If you are at the museum and you travel away from the ocean, you will go towards
14 [   ] .

Most of the floors of the car park are   **15** [   ] .

PART 3 Listening | Questions 16-20

You will hear an interview with the painter, Bridget Riley, on how her work is influenced by travelling.
For questions 16-20, choose the answer (A, B, C or D) which first best according to what you hear.

16   While on holiday, Bridget
    A. has difficulty relaxing.
    B. chooses to do things that will inspire her artistically.
    C. usually does a certain amount of painting.
    D. feels nostalgic.

17   To Bridget, walking
    A. helps her to choose the colours for her paintings.
    B. is a way for her to teach others about light and colour.
    C. was her way of forgetting.
    D. enables her to experience things in different ways.

18   During Bridget's first trip to France,
    A. she ate large amounts of food.
    B. she stayed in an impressive hotel in Paris.
    C. she read art books with great enthusiasm.
    D. she had problems getting on with her family.

19   Bridget believes that
    A. museums are best visited while on holiday.
    B. art enables you to form a deeper understanding of cultures that are foreign to you.
    C. artists can make friends with different cultures in a museum.
    D. many of the best museums are in remote places.

20   According to Bridget,
    A. Egyptian art reflects the colours of Egyptian nature.
    B. the desert inspired Ancient Egyptian theatre.
    C. she went to Egypt to find inspiration.
    D. the colours of Egypt made her feel healthier.

PART 4 Listening | Questions 21-30

You will hear five short extracts in which different people talk about the type of holiday they prefer.
You will hear the recording twice. While you listen, you must complete both tasks.

TASK ONE

For questions 21-25, choose from the list (A-H) what type of holiday each speaker went on.

A hitchhiking
B weekend break
C walking
D cruise
E skiing
F beach
G adventure
H camping

Speaker 1   21
Speaker 2   22
Speaker 3   23
Speaker 4   24
Speaker 5   25

TASK TWO

For questions 26-30, choose from the list (A-H) the reason why each speaker prefers that particular type of holiday.

A for luxury
B because of family commitments
C for the food
D because you can push yourself to be better
E to feel like one is free
F to create memories
G because of a compromise between two things
H for the location

Speaker 1   26
Speaker 2   27
Speaker 3   28
Speaker 4   29
Speaker 5   30

Test 4

Reading

PART 1 Reading   Questions 1-8

For questions 1-8, read the text below and decide which answer (A, B, C or D) best fits each gap. Mark your answers on the separate answer sheet. There is an example at the beginning (0).

Example   **0 A** traumatic   **B** enigmatic   **C** sporadic   **D** aquatic

0	A	B	C	D

Brain Gel

A gel that helps brains recover from (0).......... injuries has been developed by scientists at the Clemson University in South Carolina. The gel, which is (1).......... in liquid form at the site where the injury was sustained, (2).......... stem cell growth in the affected area. In terms of circumstances in which it might be applied, the gel has the potential to treat a wide range of head injuries, including those arising from car accidents, falls and gunshot wounds.

Serious brain injuries are (3).......... difficult to recover from on account of the fact that the affected tissue can swell up considerably, which causes additional (4).......... damage to the surrounding cells. Existing treatments do little more than attempt to limit secondary damage and are relatively (5).......... , certainly when it comes to repairing the damaged cells, so the discovery of a gel which stimulates cell repair is being (6).......... as revolutionary.

Despite the wave of excitement now running through medical circles, it is important to note that results so far are (7).......... solely on observations of the effects of the gel on laboratory rats. The development of the treatment is very much still in its (8).......... stages and human testing is expected to be some three years or more away yet.

	A		B		C		D	
1.	implanted		instilled		injected		imposed
2.	motivates		vitalises		stimulates		mobilises
3.	notionally		incidentally		notoriously		increasingly
4.	corresponding		collateral		coincident		dependent
5.	integrated		ineffective		incompetent		unproductive
6.	heralded		advertised		promised		ushered
7.	based		rested		discovered		stationed
8.	penultimate		preliminary		concluding		fundamental

PART 2 Reading | **Questions 9-16**

For questions 9-16 read the text below and think of the word which best fits each gap. Use only one word in each space. There is an example at the beginning (0).

Example: | 0 | LITTLE

The Emergence of British Pop

Before 1960, the UK pop scene offered (0) *little* of substance. A faint shadow of its American counterpart, it could boast (9)................................. the questionable talents of sanitised singers like Cliff Richard and Tommy Steele. But then along came the revolution; fizzing out of the teen-oriented coffee bars and the budding club circuit came the likes of Korner and Barber as R&B emerged. It was not long before 'bluephoria' had taken (10)................................. and the blues and R&B circuit quickly evolved with bands of the calibre of the Rolling Stones and the Graham Bond Organization shaking things (11)................................. in London.

But the capital did not have a monopoly as far as new talent was concerned - (12)................................. from it. The north was awakening, too, and soon the Beat groups would arrive, taking the music world by (13)................................. . Acts such as the Animals and the Beatles were formed, the latter needing no introduction, of course.
It wasn't long before the tables had (14)................................. ; American pop was soon playing second fiddle to Brit-style bands.

The Beatles, championing the cause, took British popular music to new levels of success. Before (15)................................. , the world couldn't get enough of this plucky quartet. 'Beatlemania' had taken hold. John, Paul, Ringo and George could do no (16)................................. .

PART 3 Reading | **Questions 17-24**

For questions 17-24, read the text below. Use the word given in capitals at the end of the lines to form a word that fits in the space in the same line. There is an example at the beginning (0).
Write your answers **IN CAPITAL LETTERS** on the separate answer sheet.

Example: | 0 | inaccessible

The Antarctic Ice Marathon

There is no other race quite like it; no other race in a place so (0) *inaccessible*; no other race which   ACCESS
puts the body through a(n) (17)................................. test of such extremes. The Antarctic Ice Marathon was the   ENDURE
brainchild of Richard Donovan, whose company, Polar Running Adventures, gives runners the opportunity to
(18)................................. in a race through the barren wasteland that is the snow-covered Union Glacier.   TAKE

Last year, there were some 34 participants in the race, and, this time, the number of (19).................................   ENTER
is expected to be higher still; such has been the level of interest shown by members of the public, amateur
and professional athletes and the media alike.

But, while the prospect of being part of as unique an experience as the Antarctic Ice Marathon is seems,
on the face of it, a rather (20)................................. notion, those considering putting their names in the mix would   AGREE
do well to be (21)................................. of just how intense and demanding, both physically and psychologically, the MIND
event can be.

You will be cut off completely from civilization, with not even a penguin there to cheer you on, and
you may have to face temperatures dipping considerably lower than the levels your body would be   CUSTOM/
(22)................................. to dealing with, not to mention the (23)................................. of fine weather - think instead   PROBABLE
near whiteout conditions and zero (24)................................. .   VISIBLE

But, if you still fancy giving it a go, get in touch with Richard and he can make your dream (or nightmare)
come true ...

For questions 25-30, complete the second sentence so that it has a similar meaning to the first sentence, using the word given. Do not change the word given. You must use between three and eight words, including the word given. Here is an example (0).

Example:

0   Mick will give you lots of excuses for being late but don't believe any of them.

matter

No .... Mick gives you for being late, don't believe any of them.

Write only the missing words on the separate answer sheet.

25. Do you mind if I change the channel?

objection

Do you .... the channel?

26. Give me a phone call when you arrive, even if it is after my bedtime.

whether

No .... when you arrive, give me a phone call.

27. A lack of match practice is threatening to ruin the player's chances of qualifying.

under

The player's .... a lack of match practice.

28. Her father made it clear that he would not be discussing the matter any further.

open

Her father made it clear that .... discussion.

29. The prisoner was led to the dock by an armed officer.

way

The prisoner .... under armed escort.

30. The lawyer for the defence suggested the witness was not telling the truth.

doubt

The defence lawyer .... version of events.

PART 5   Reading | **Questions 31-36**

You are going to read an article about the Dead Sea. For questions 31-36, choose the answer (A, B, C or D) which you think fits best according to the text. Mark your answers on the separate answer sheet.

The Devil's Sea

Although, in modern history, we have been slow to recognise the exceptionality of the Dead Sea area, that intensely salinated body of water separating Israel and Jordan, hostile to all forms of life bar a few microscopic species of bacteria and a smattering of miniscule fungi, we seem, today at least, far more aware and appreciative of its, well, usefulness, not to mention the very uniqueness that defines the place, being, as it is, both the lowest land elevation on the planet and the deepest hypersaline lake or inland sea of its kind.

In fact, it was not until 1848 that the 'Sea of the Devil', as it was then popularly known, piqued the curiosity of Westerners, when a group of US navy officers exploring the area were at once fascinated and perplexed by the phenomenon that lay before them. Their passing interest aside, however, the first real exploitation of the area did not begin until more than seventy years later when, under the British Mandate for Palestine, Britain began to tap into the area's abundant mineral wealth for the first time, leading to, at one point, nearly half of the entire potash needs of the British Commonwealth being sourced from the region.

That the Dead Sea region was ignored for so much of modern history is best explained by its reputation; after all, people reasoned, if its waters were hostile to all forms of life (as was presumed until the presence of diminutive bacterial and fungal life was confirmed by scientists in the last twenty years), it was surely an area best avoided; an area unfit for mankind to venture into and explore. Besides, the name itself is hardly reassuring, nor are the other variants by which it has, at one time or another, been known – 'The Devil's Sea', 'The Stinking Sea' and so on. Of course, other factors also delayed the area's exploitation, not least of which, the harsh climes of the Middle East, where, in summer, temperatures in the mid- to high-30s are not uncommon, nor is it so rare to see the thermometer registering above 40. Another factor was the barren, rocky terrain. However, the luxuries of modern roads and air-conditioned vehicles have since put paid to these concerns.

Still, it is odd to reflect on for just how long the region was left in splendid isolation, particularly given the fact that in ancient times, as far back as the 4th century BC, it was not by any means ignored. Indeed, the great Greek philosopher Aristotle is known to have made mention of the sea's physical properties, as are other luminaries of the period, such as Galen and Pliny. The Nabataeans, an ancient North Arabian tribe, were not slow to recognise the area's potential either, collecting bitumen from the surface of the water and selling it to the Egyptians, for whom it was a vital ingredient in the process of embalming. This particular Dead Sea industry continued well into Roman times. The area was also a favoured retreat for religious ascetics and political fugitives, and figures such as the future King David, King Herod, John the Baptist and Jesus are all thought to have taken refuge along its shoreline. Nevertheless, from classical times up until the US Navy's visit little more than a century and a half ago, the Dead Sea region was by and large shunned.

But perhaps this was just as well, for ever since our attention has turned to this inland sea, and we have begun to grasp the extent of its healing properties and the sheer abundance of mineral wealth it bequeaths, as is our wont as humans when it comes to our treatment of all the gifts Mother Earth bestows perhaps, we have been none too kind to the region, and indeed, some would say, have treated it with outright and careless disdain.

Though supplemented by several smaller rivers and streams, the Dead Sea is fed in the main by the Jordan River. The inflow, of course, having nowhere to go, were it not for the intense heat of the sun, which produces a high rate of evaporation, the sea itself would rise in perpetuum, swallowing up large swathes of the surrounding coastline. But, as it is, the evaporation rate keeps the volume of water in the sea fairly constant and also gives it its uniquely saline character. Water which flows into the sea is not dissimilar in terms of mineral concentration to any waterflow, but the intense evaporation results in the concentration levels of minerals within the lake-water itself climbing sharply, which explains why the Dead Sea, with salt levels of around 30%, is ten times more saline than the ocean. Here, in the case of the Dead Sea, as in so many instances, nature is in perfect balance, the water cycle ensuring the status quo is maintained, and that enough water is fed into the Dead Sea to maintain its water level, while enough escapes so as to preserve the coastline. Or at least that was the case - until man interfered.

Today, however, the future of the Dead Sea is in jeopardy. Together, Jordan, Syria and Israel divert more than 1.3 billion cubic metres of water from the Jordan River annually to satisfy their needs for domestic consumption purposes, as well as for irrigation and other water-guzzling activities, and, while it is true that the people must eat and drink – so no one denies the importance of water used for consumption and crops – what is also becoming more and more apparent is that the Dead Sea is being starved of liquid replenishment, and, as it starves, it is slowly but surely disappearing.

In the last 30 years, the sea's surface area has shrunk by almost one-third, and its depth has fallen by 25 metres. The receding shoreline is also exposing rock and soil high in brine deposits to rainwater and freshwater runoff, and these brine deposits are gradually being dissolved, causing a phenomenon whereby thousands of sinkholes are appearing along the western shore. In what has been termed The Dead Sea's Revenge, a number of these openings have resulted in fatalities, and the main road linking Ein Gedi - one of Israel's most attractive oases, known for its spas offering packages of mud treatments and Dead Sea bathing - with the rest of the country is now dangerously close to some of the sinkhole openings, which suggests its days of car-ferrying may be numbered.

Perhaps, The Devil's Sea would have done well to have kept its inglorious reputation, for, having rediscovered this natural wonder in recent years, mankind now, sadly, seems hell-bent on destroying it.

31. **What do we learn in the first two paragraphs?**
    A. Throughout modern history right up into present times, people have always been slow to appreciate how exceptional an area the Dead Sea is.
    B. The Dead Sea is home to virulent strains of bacteria and fungi that are extremely hostile to all other forms of life.
    C. The first time in modern history a sustained interest in the Dead Sea was shown was when the U.S. Navy began to exploit the area.
    D. The Dead Sea is only home to a few diminutive life forms and was largely spared any significant human interference until the early part of the twentieth century.

32. **Which of the following was NOT a factor which contributed to the Dead Sea being ignored for a significant part of modern history?**
    A. the generally-held belief that the absence of living creatures in the area was a sign that it should be steered clear of
    B. the various unflattering titles by which the sea has been known
    C. the features of the rocky landscape which made travel difficult
    D. the infrequency with which temperatures in the region reached the mid-to-high 30s or above

33. **In classical history, the Dead Sea**
    A. was a site of great religious and political significance.
    B. was occupied by a naval force for more than a century and a half.
    C. provided a place of refuge for devoutly religious people and fleeing political figures.
    D. was a favoured holiday retreat for both political and religious figures alike.

34. **The intensity of the sun's heat**
    A. serves to stabilise the level of the Dead Sea and give it its salty character.
    B. produces a high rate of evaporation in the rivers that feed the Dead Sea.
    C. causes the Dead Sea to expand and swallow up huge areas of coastline.
    D. keeps the volume of water in the Dead Sea fairly constant and the mineral concentration similar to that of most other waterflows.

35. **What does the writer say about the activities of Israel, Jordan and Syria?**
    A. He accuses them of pumping over a billion cubic metres of water out of the lake every year.
    B. He questions their right to divert water away from the Dead Sea to use for consumption and crop irrigation.
    C. They are diverting huge quantities of water from the sea's main water supply source, which is having a marked effect on the water level of the sea itself.
    D. They are pumping water from the Dead Sea into the Jordan River for consumption and crop purposes, which is causing the sea itself to reduce in size.

36. **What does the writer imply in the second last paragraph?**
    A. The main road to Ein Gedi will not be in use much longer.
    B. The surface area of the sea is likely to shrink and its depth fall dramatically over the coming 30 years.
    C. Rainwater is the cause of the sinkhole phenomenon as it produces large deposits of brine.
    D. Ein Gedi is perilously close to being destroyed by sink holes.

PART 6 Reading | **Questions 37-43**

You are going to read an extract from a newspaper article. Seven paragraphs have been removed from the extract. Choose from the paragraphs A-H the one which fits each gap (37-43). There is one extra paragraph you do not need to use. Mark your answers on the separate answer sheet.

Land on Fire

SJ Haughton takes us on a journey through a land of spectacular geology
where the raw power of nature is evident most everywhere you look.

Iceland is, in many respects, a forgotten land as far as the tourist trade goes. Location wise, it can't make up its mind whether it wants to be near America or Europe, and ends up a fair distance away from both – just far enough, in fact, to put off many would-be travellers who balk at the idea of five hours or more spent on a budget flight from the UK, manoeuvring into all sorts of contorted positions in an effort to get comfortable, on the way to its capital, Reykjavik. In any case, most reason, there can't be altogether much of anything to do there, right?

37

But, be warned, do the latter and you will soon conclude that your money could well have been much better spent had you only had the patience to endure the slightly more cramped and ordinary surrounds of a budget carrier for what is, at the end of the day, but a few hours – the trip to Iceland is hardly long-haul now, is it?

38

Sure, the bright lights of the city are a tad invasive, but they do not spoil the horizon. There! Now you've spotted that rather peculiar-looking piece of land in the top right-hand corner of your view; a black expanse that seems to have no end. And how it rises up in the centre; a permanent white-powder gracing its craterous peak.

Welcome to the lava fields. Lava? Yes. Or didn't you know? Well, better get used to it; you're only on one of the most geologically temperamental land masses this planet of ours has ever dreamt up; ever changing, Iceland's terrain is truly unique; no other European country has such an abundance of geological features of this kind; you will soon find yourself exploring deep craters, lava fields reminiscent in their barrenness of JR Tolkien's doom-filled Mordor, land of the devil-creature Sauron, and cone-shaped mountains whose chimneys bellow smoke on a disturbingly regular basis – often enough to keep you on your toes and patently aware of the fact that things could kick off at any moment.

39

It is said that 60% of Icelanders believe in elves; well, it is not hard to see why – you half expect one to pop up in front of you any minute, emerging from the steamy horizon.

40

Iceland is no one-trick pony when it comes to natural features. What you saw in that first glance at the horizon was but one section of this patchwork quilt. The gods have sown on many more which you will soon discover. But put your hankering for adventure to one side a moment, and cast your gaze a little closer to where you are now standing; the capital is but a stone's throw away and is deserving of at least a little of your attention.

41

The first stop on your journey, then, is about 50 km away – roughly half an hour in your newly-acquired wagon. The historic midtown and harbour area is quaint and atmospheric. Park your car, and get out and walk; this is one of the few times you won't really need it. Visit the National Gallery and Culture House, and the National Museum, too, if you've time to fit all that in, but allow yourself just one afternoon to do so; you're not here for the museums or to admire the traditional architecture; these are only momentary distractions, albeit very nice ones. Museums we can find anywhere, but volcanoes and the like we cannot.

42

Bed down in the lodgings of your choice – there is something for every budget – for a cosy night's sleep, but pry yourself away from that soft down-feather pillow as early as your strength can muster your limbs into action once the sun is up; now the adventure begins.

43

But at least it's organised chaos, and the locals have everything well in hand, even managing to harness her fiery creations to serve their own purposes; almost 80% of the country's energy needs are sourced from the natural forces at work on the land itself.

To be continued in next week's travel supplement.

A

Well, that largely depends on one's perspective, as I discovered on a recent visit. And it turns out that, for the outdoorsy type of person, the Atlantic island offers a wealth of opportunities to explore. Sure, either you suck it up and endure the dreaded cost-cutter flight to get there, and disembark from the plane a little on the sore side but none really the worse for wear, or you pay top dollar for that semblance of travel chic you are looking for.

B

Heading inland, just north of the capital, you will come to Þingvellir National Park, a broad rift valley where the effects of opposing tectonic plates pulling away from each other are immediately visible and provide one with a real sense of the geological mayhem playing out underfoot. Here in Iceland, the Earth's crust is thinner than anywhere else; this land is brand-new in geological terms, and is still being shaped and remodelled by that most unpredictable of artists, Mother Nature herself, who seems intent on taking out her fury on the young land, and whipping it up into a firestorm of volcanic and geothermal bedlam.

C

But whether you emerge penny savvy or penniless, take a moment to pat yourself on the back; you'll have made a good choice of destination either way. And, in that same moment, if you are not pushed and hustled into returning to the grim reality of making your way towards customs prematurely by those eager beaver types disembarking behind you, pause and take in your surrounds. Already, it seems to me, you will be starting to grasp what lies in store on this gem of an island.

D

Or perhaps, on second thoughts, stay put for now. Tomorrow is, after all, another day. Though there is much still to do, you have factored this in - haven't you? You are, of course, here for at least another eight to ten days, right? I should certainly hope so, for we have yet but barely scratched the surface of this splendiferous isle.

E

But there are no foul creatures here – well, unless you have the misfortune to run into a lone roaming polar bear - rare visitors to Iceland, but probably best avoided. And nor is Iceland the grim cauldron of hate and fear that it superficially resembles; barren though the lava fields may be, their beauty is inescapable. The black rock, contrasted against the lying snow, is a sight to behold. And the deep holes in the ground venting sulphur - steamy chasms scattered about the countryside for miles around - combine with the snowy lava fields to create an almost mystical landscape.

F

End your sojourn with a delightful sea-food dinner at one of the city's excellent fish restaurants. This is an island after all, and they have been cooking lobster and all varieties of fruits de mer for a very, very long time; there may be no Michelin stars hanging over the doorway, but a good meal here is the equal of any served in the over-priced and pretentious haunts of Europe's great capitals; in fact, the celebrity chefs of Paris and London could even learn a thing or two from their Icelandic cousins, if they weren't so busy listening in self-congratulatory mode to the sounds of their own voices interminably playing on re-runs of cooking shows on cable T.V.

G

A nudge from behind … back to the now with you, quickly; you can't dawdle too long. Having allowed yourself to get lost in the moment, you awaken from your daydream to realise that there are still steps to manoeuvre and still a plane to be disembarked; there is a holiday to begin. That you have been so enraptured by the sight of the lava fields from afar is a good sign because believe me, if you thought that was impressive, you are going to be truly wowed by what lies ahead.

H

So turn the key and start up the engine of your rental car – and if you haven't pre-booked one in advance of your arrival, then trust me, now is no time for thriftiness; fork out the extra few quid required to secure a decent motor; there is only one way to explore this island, and it is with pedal underfoot – unless you fancy embarking on a journey as epic as Scott's Antarctic quest (and good luck with that by the way…).

PART 7 Reading | **Questions 44-53**

You are going to read an article about some popular outdoor tourist destinations in Canada. For questions 44-53, choose from the destinations (A-E). Each destination may be chosen more than once.

Mark your answers on the separate answer sheet.

To which destination does each statement relate?

Although this area is rich in natural beauty, the majority of tourists only come to visit during three specific months of the year for an unrelated reason. **44** ☐

In this area, visitors only have the opportunity to play a particular sport during one season each year. **45** ☐

A spectacle which takes place in this region is only known to the few people who thoroughly research the area. **46** ☐

This area sees a huge influx of people at a particular time each year. **47** ☐

This area affords visitors an excellent opportunity to partake in a variety of water sports and activities. **48** ☐

This place is known to attract visitors who are on a romantic vacation. **49** ☐

This destination, or a large part thereof, straddles two separate countries. **50** ☐
 51 ☐

This area offers a variety of terrain such that it is suitable for people of different levels of ability. **52** ☐
 53 ☐

Confront your fears and face your challenges

Churchill   A

Churchill, Manitoba, has much to offer in the way of sightseeing, and its natural surrounds are truly spectacular, but its beauty is nothing but a side-show; the polar bears are the main event in these parts, Churchill being the unofficial polar bear capital of the world. Every year, from October to early December, these giant carnivores gather at the mouth of the Churchill River in Hudson Bay and wait patiently until the sea freezes over to enable them to resume seal-hunting again. The town of Churchill has a mere 900 permanents residents, but, during peak bear-spotting season, the population swells to more than 10,000, as visitors from near and far come to see the estimated 1,200 of these cuddly-looking but decidedly lethal beasts that gather around the town each year. Sadly though, most of the visitors, once they have seen their share of bears and taken the obligatory been-there-done-it photo, head home without even pausing to scan the horizon for the other spectacular creature that can be seen in relative abundance here, the Beluga, whose sleek profile is frequently spotted breaking the surface of the water in the bay, offering up a perfect opportunity for whale-watching that only those who have really done their homework will ever get to take advantage of.

Banff   B

Banff was designated Canada's first national park way back in 1885 in recognition of the fact that it is an area of truly outstanding natural beauty. Its jagged peaks set against the never-ending light-blue skyline exemplify what the wild and rugged, and remarkably vast range that is the Canadian Rockies is all about. Every year, the park attracts around four million visitors, lured there by the promise of postcard views and abundant wildlife. Banff is home to some 54 mammalian species, from the impressive but harmless moose and elk, to the more lethal cougar, black bear and grizzly bear. The park is also home to a thriving adventure sports industry, and offers first-rate hiking trails with sufficient variety of terrain so as to ensure that both the novice and experienced trekker are kept satisfied.

Niagara Falls   C

A raging torrent whose fame is such that little if any introduction is necessary, there is a very good reason why Niagara Falls, or, be more precise, Canadian Falls, the horseshoe-shaped section of the gorge this side of the border, is visited by such large numbers of tourists every year, and that is the simple truth that the scene which greets you on arrival is one of the few genuinely awe-inspiring spectacles you are ever likely to have the privilege to behold. The falls have proved an irresistible temptation for many a daredevil over the years, too, with tightrope walker Nik Wallenda being the most recent case in point - his successful crossing in June 2012 was reported widely in the international media. But for those of us who aren't inclined towards acts of such reckless insanity, there is an alternative to the perilous rope-walk which offers an equally noteworthy view; the river-boat ride, which takes you just close enough beneath the gushing torrent to be momentarily deafened by its roar - and you get a free shower into the bargain! A honeymooner's as well as nature-lover's paradise, Niagara should form part of every visitor's itinerary.

The Laurentians   D

Just north of Montreal, the distinctly Gallic feel of Mont-Tremblant, a European-style resort in the heart of the Laurentian Mountains, is typical of the villages of the region. The range itself is an all-season paradise which is at its best perhaps during late autumn when the forests explode into a symphony of colour. The area attracts nature- and adventure-lovers alike because, as well as the resplendence of its natural canvass, it can also boast some of the best ski terrain in North America (with slopes to cater for every level of enthusiast) and excellent golf - the main attraction of which is playing against this stunning backdrop no doubt, though the courses are not too shabby either – in the summer season.

The Great Lakes   E

Known for their diversity and beauty, and for their disproportionately large contribution to the Earth's ecology, the five great lakes combined comprise the largest body of freshwater on the planet. Their volume is distributed more or less equally between the States and Canada, with the exception of Lake Michigan which is completely contained within the former country. Their combined surface area is larger than that of England, Scotland and Wales put together. All five lakes are interconnected with their primary outlet being the Saint Lawrence River, which flows through Quebec and eventually empties out into the North Atlantic. Bearing in mind the sheer size of these bodies of water, few visitors can afford themselves the time required to see all five, but a stop at any of the various national parks dotted along their shores is very worthwhile, and an excellent excuse to take in some water-based activities, too, with yachting, canoeing, scuba diving and much more to choose from.

PART 1   Writing   **Question 1**

Read the two texts below.

Write an essay summarising and evaluating the key points from both texts. Use your own words throughout as far as possible, and include your own ideas in your answers.

Write your answer in **240-280** words.

1.

Social Sham

The extent to which young people have become dependent on computer-type technology is patently evident in their near total inability to articulate themselves properly anymore. The social incompetence exhibited by many of today's youth is symptomatic of hours and days spent hunched up in front of the computer screen each week, playing online games with virtual friends and posting meaningless status updates on their 'social' network to their enormous virtual cliques, the members of which they have little if any genuine social interaction with, making a mockery of the very premise on which these so-called 'social' networks are built.

Communication Revolution

Today's youth is championing the most significant change in the way we interact that society has ever seen. No longer are the limits of time and place relevant to communication. By embracing new technology, young people have cast these limits to one side. Today, we are talking to each other more than ever before. Texting, calling, video-calling, emailing, posting, messaging, skyping and so forth keep us connected with friends, work colleagues and family twenty-four, seven. We have never been so zoned in to what is happening around us. The phenomenon of the information age has created a more informed youth, capable of meaningful interaction on a level that was until now unachievable.

Write your **essay**.

PART 2   Writing   **Questions 2-4**

Write an answer to **one** of the questions **2-4** in this part. Write your answer in **280-320** words in an appropriate style on the separate answer sheet. Put the question number in the box at the top of the answer sheet.

2. A literary magazine is running a series of reviews of books that feature sports or sports persons as a main theme, and which would be of interest to young people with aspirations of pursuing a career in sport. You decide to send in a review in which you describe a book with a sporting theme which you have read, mentioning what aspects of the content you enjoyed and why you would recommend the book to young readers with a keen interest in sport.

   Write your **review**.

3. An international travel magazine is running a series of articles on alternatives to the very popular and crowded tourist destinations most of us visit each year. The magazine has invited readers to send in articles briefly describing a memorable holiday they spent in an unusual destination, explaining the advantages of holidaying in less popular places and whether in general they think avoiding the crowds when on holiday results in a more satisfying experience.

   Write your **article**.

4. A careers fair was recently held in your town for local and international educational institutes to promote their courses on offer to school leavers. You have been asked to write a report on the careers fair for your school website. You should briefly describe the event and identify two or three unusual further education course options promoted there. You should also evaluate the extent to which such events can adequately inform young people about the range of study options available and help them to make the right decisions about their futures.

   Write your **report**.

Listening

PART 1 **Listening** **Questions 1-6**

You will hear three different extracts. For questions 1-6, choose the answer (A, B, or C) which fits best according to what you hear. There are two questions for each extract.

EXTRACT 1

You hear a consultant in accounting and taxation law talking about the tax treatment of couples and civil partners.

1. What is significant about the date mentioned by the speaker?
   A. civil partnerships could not be legally registered before it
   B. all civil partners had to legally register after it
   C. civil partners registered after it are taxed like married couples

2. What can couples where only one partner works do to reduce their tax bill?
   A. transfer assets to the ownership of the working partner
   B. transfer the partner who is not working's tax allowance to the working partner
   C. transfer assets that earn money to the non-working partner

EXTRACT 2

You hear two Politics students discussing a new type of school system supported by the government.

3. What is the male speaker's point about government funding?
   A. the state should only fund schools it is in control of
   B. the state should be allowed to inspect schools it funds
   C. government funding helps broaden the curriculum of Free Schools

4. What does the male speaker say about Free Schools run by religious orders?
   A. only students of the order's religion can attend
   B. such schools segregate their classes by religion
   C. most students wanting to attend will be of the same religion

EXTRACT 3

You hear a lecturer in photography talking to a group of students about different types of cameras.

5. What can we imply about amateur photography today?
   A. the use of digital cameras is in decline
   B. digital SLR cameras are the preferred type for amateurs
   C. all types of SLR cameras are equally popular

6. In what respect are traditional film-dependent cameras still superior?
   A. image quality
   B. ease of use
   C. functionality

PART 2 Listening   **Questions 7-15**

You will hear a scientist talking about an important discovery in molecular biology.
For questions 7-15 complete the sentences with a word or short phrase.

As well as contributing to the discovery of new techniques, the speaker suggests the double helix

discovery [7 _____] a new field of science.

Watson and Crick were jointly awarded a Nobel Prize open to people with a background in

[8 _____] .

Oswald Avery proved conclusively that hereditary [9 _____] was

contained in human DNA.

Crick and Watson were adept at using the discoveries of [10 _____]

for their own purposes in investigating the composition of DNA.

Such was their focus and determination to discover the secrets of genetics that their success was

almost a [11 _____] .

Their [12 _____] put them at an advantage in their quest, though

they also relied on their intuition and persistence, and had no shortage of good fortune.

Alexander Todd had already found out the roles of certain [13 _____]

in the composition of DNA.

Chemist Linus Pauling's innovative technique of [14 _____] was

employed by Crick and Watson in their research.

Jerry Donohue's observation that there was a flaw in conventional theory of chemistry paved the way

for Crick and Watson's [15 _____] .

PART 3 Listening Questions 16-20

You will hear part of a discussion on a radio talk show between a professor, Max Mantle, a representative of students, Pauline O'Boyle, and their host with regard to a recent increase in university fees. For questions 16-20, choose the answer (A, B, C or D) which fits best according to what you hear.

16 How does Pauline O'Boyle feel about the official announcement on university fees?
   A. She is relieved that they are finally going up.
   B. She is surprised that the announcement was not made months ago.
   C. She is pleased that the news was not as bad as some had predicted.
   D. It was pretty much along the lines of what she had expected.

17 What does Max Mantle think the public is not aware of?
   A. the considerable amount of government funding universities receive
   B. how much universities rely on student fees
   C. the lack of grant aid offered to third-level students
   D. the extent to which the U.K. education system is mocked in Europe

18 What does Pauline O'Boyle say about student grants?
   A. only grammar- and private-school students may apply for them
   B. applicants from grammar and private schools are given preference

   C. very few state-school students manage to qualify for them
   D. they should be made grade-dependent so as to be fairer

19 Pauline believes that universities
   A. should do more to look after the interests of their professors.
   B. offer terms of employment that are counterproductive.
   C. should ask the government for more hand-outs.
   D. will only become more efficiently run if salaries and conditions improve.

20 What is the last point made by Max Mantle?
   A. lecturers' salaries and terms of employment have been reviewed
   B. lecturers need to review their salaries and terms of employment carefully
   C. reducing lecturers' pay by one or two thousand pounds will help to solve the problem
   D. the existence of overpaid lecturers is not a significant part of the problem

PART 4 Listening Questions 21-30

You will hear five short extracts in which employees express their views on overtime and their work colleagues. You will hear the recording twice. While you listen, you must complete both tasks.

TASK ONE

For questions 21-25, choose from the list (A-H) how each speaker feels about doing overtime.

A they enjoy spending their evenings at work

B it is necessary because they are a health care worker

C they refuse to do overtime on financial grounds

D they do it to put some savings aside

E they do it to impress their employer

F they don't mind doing voluntary or unpaid overtime

G they always put their family first

H they cannot do it for health reasons

Speaker 1		21
Speaker 2		22
Speaker 3		23
Speaker 4		24
Speaker 5		25

TASK TWO

For questions 26-30, choose from the list (A-H) what is said about the speaker's work colleagues.

A they are very united in general as a team

B they are somewhat jealous of the speaker's performance

C they never leave tasks outstanding until the next day

D they are good at managing their workloads

E they are quite rude to each other

F they tend to have a lot of disagreements

G they do not push themselves to work very hard

H some of their jobs may be under threat

Speaker 1		26
Speaker 2		27
Speaker 3		28
Speaker 4		29
Speaker 5		30

Test 5

Reading

PART 1 Reading | **Questions 1-8**

For questions 1-8, read the text below and decide which answer (A, B, C or D) best fits each gap. Mark your answers on the separate answer sheet. There is an example at the beginning (0).

Example   **0 A** infamous   **B** reputable   **C** popular   **D** sheer

Dinosaur Provincial Park

Located in the (0).......... badlands of southeastern Alberta, the park is undoubtedly best-known for its (1)..........
fossil beds, where some 35 different species of dinosaur from the Late Cretaceous period have so far been
identified. The area was (2).......... a UNESCO world heritage site some three decades ago, not just on account
of its paleontological value, but also due to the (3).......... of animal and plant life to which it is home.

The Red Deer River runs through the present-day park, creating a habitat in which willows and cottonwoods
(4).......... . Antelope and a type of deer whose name is lent to the aforementioned intersecting river graze on
the grassy plains of the area, which is also (5).......... to other mammalian species such as the predatory coyote
and the rabbit - the coyote's main food source in the area, which also supports more than 150 species of
birds.

Dinosaur fossils were first discovered here nearly a century and a half ago, but large-scale (6).......... did not
begin for another 30-odd years. Significant (7).......... include a near-complete skeleton of Albertosaurus libratus,
a member of the tyrannosaur family, and a complete skull of Centrosaurus apertus, a horned dinosaur that
lived a(n) (8) .... 75 million years ago.

1.	A extensive	B	thorough	C	expanded	D	protracted
2.	A designated	B	allocated	C	apportioned	D	nominated
3.	A uniformity	B	diversity	C	extent	D	fluctuation
4.	A thrive	B	progress	C	improve	D	elevate
5.	A home	B	range	C	ground	D	open
6.	A explorations	B	excavations	C	examinations	D	extrapolations
7.	A works	B	catches	C	assets	D	finds
8.	A regarded	B	anticipated	C	predicted	D	estimated

For questions 9-16 read the text below and think of the word which best fits each gap. Use only one word in each space. There is an example at the beginning (0).

Example: | **0** | **AVERAGE** |

From Royalist to Republican

Erskine Childers was not what you would call your **(0)**.....**average**......... Irish freedom fighter. A Briton by birth, and a proud **(9)**.................................. at that for most of the early years of his life, Childers was a decorated soldier of the British Admiralty **(10)**................................ had demonstrated unwavering commitment and loyalty to both king and country. And yet, somewhere along the way, disillusionment **(11)**................................ in.

While it is difficult to pinpoint the precise moment when doubt started to creep into Childers' mind **(12)**................................ to whether his loyalty was misguided, what was essentially a complete philosophy shift - a total realignment of ideals — did occur. Childers went from **(13)**................................ a royalist to a staunch nationalist, obsessed with the cause of Irish freedom.

He befriended the **(14)**................................ of Eamon DeVelera and Michael Collins, key figures in the Irish Republican camp, and even went so far as to ship illegal armaments to the leaders of the ill-fated Easter Rising of 1916, which was easily put **(15)**................................ by the British army.

Later, he would fight on the side of the Irish rebels in the War of Independence, until an uneasy truce was agreed between Britain and Ireland. Eventually, a treaty was signed partitioning the country. For Childers, by now totally devoted to the cause of Irish freedom and the notion of a united Ireland, partition was **(16)**................................ bitter a pill to swallow.

For questions 17-24, read the text below. Use the word given in capitals at the end of the lines to form a word that fits in the space in the same line. There is an example at the beginning (0).
Write your answers **IN CAPITAL LETTERS** on the separate answer sheet.

Example: | **0** | **transplant** |

New Treatment Provides Hope for Older Women Looking to have Children

A recent breakthrough in ovarian **(0)** *transplant* treatment is what scientists are claiming is the first   PLANT
step towards developing the **(17)**................................ to postpone menopause by a decade or more, which would   CAPABLE
see women well into their late 50s potentially being given the opportunity to **(18)**................................ a success-   GO
ful term of pregnancy at the end of which they would have as good a chance as any of producing a healthy
young child.

The new technique involves the **(19)**................................ of parts of a healthy young ovary, which are then put   MOVE
into **(20)**................................ to be transplanted back into the patient's body decades later, **(21)**................................   STORE/
her capacity to conceive for what is potentially an indefinite period. Once perfected, the treatment could be   LONG
so effective as to **(22)**................................ women of sixty-plus years to give birth.   ABLE

Of course, already the discovery has caused its fair share of controversy. Critics are very worried that it
could, in future, lead to a trend whereby elderly women have children at such an advanced age that they are
far from properly equipped to perform their **(23)**................................ duties.   PARENT

But, such a scenario aside, the **(24)**................................ does offer a sense of hope to women, who, for what-   TREAT
ever reason, only start to think about having kids in their late thirties or early forties, because, in a sense, the
biological clock will not seem like it is ticking so ominously anymore.

PART 4 Reading | **Questions 25-30**

For questions 25-30, complete the second sentence so that it has a similar meaning to the first sentence, using the word given. Do not change the word given. You must use between three and eight words, including the word given. Here is an example (0).

Example:

0   I think I just saw Frankie for a split second driving past in a Ferrari no less.   caught

I think I just .... for a split second driving past in a Ferrari no less.

Write only the missing words on the separate answer sheet. | 0 | caught sight of Frankie |

25. Jackie really has no idea of the difficulty of driving to London during rush hour.

how

Little does .... drive to London during rush hour.

26. The applicant's cover letter impressed his prospective employers immediately on viewing it.

sooner

No .... than were his prospective employers impressed by it.

27. I felt relaxed at my boyfriend's house because his parents treated me like part of the family.

ease

My boyfriend's parents .... treating me like part of the family.

28. The team was divided over who should be chosen to lead the expedition.

choice

The .... dividing the team.

29. The crash victim was beyond help when emergency services reached her.

whatsoever

There .... do on reaching the crash victim.

30. His childhood piano teacher impressed him in a way he would never forget.

lasting

His childhood piano teacher .... him.

PART 5 Reading | Questions 31-36

You are going to read an article about Tayrona National Park in Colombia. For questions 31-36, choose the answer (A, B, C or D) which you think fits best according to the text. Mark your answers on the separate answer sheet.

Tayrona National Park, Colombia

Stretching for some 85 km along the pristine Colombian coastline north of Taganga, a visit to Tayrona National Park is an unquestionably memorable experience, guaranteed to make you feel at once full and appreciative of life. Its tropical dry forests boast a fascinating array of wildlife, from black howler monkeys and red woodpeckers to iguana lizards and those most secretive of big cats: jaguars. But Tayrona has developed a reputation as something of a tourism hotspot not just because of its abundant and diverse wildlife but as much for the smattering of golden, sandy beaches dotted along its Caribbean coastline.

The entry-route for most visitors is via Santa Marta, the Magdalena region's capital, and with flights there continuing to be priced more and more keenly each year, this is a further incentive to travel for would-be visitors, if not the actual deal-maker. Buses bound for Tayrona depart from the city centre every half-hour, delivering passengers to the park entrance, and from there a walk of roughly four kilometres is required to get to the heart of the reserve. Other travel options are, of course, also available; taxi prices are by no means extortionate here and the trip from Santa Marta won't leave your wallet feeling prematurely light, which is important with your holiday barely underway and so much of merit yet to do and worth paying for. Car-hire prices are not prohibitive either, though you will need something a little more robust than the typical rent-a-car 1.3 litre.

A word of warning though; don't come expecting to find yourself laying pool-side at some plush Caribbean hotel for your 'week-to-ten-days' (which, incidentally, is not nearly enough time to do this trip justice); the park interior is a conservation area, and not just in name; officials take their work seriously. The only overnighting options are the campsites and the very modest and aptly-named eco-tourist hammock huts. For those who like their mod cons and for those for whom the word holiday equates to indulgence, better, perhaps, to travel in and out of the park by day and stay in one of the surrounding townships, which offer lodgings of a more luxurious nature.

Within the confines of the park, heed warning signs where present; to ignore them would be foolish at best but could quite easily have more permanent and fatal consequences. The Arrecifes area, for example, while quick to beguile you with its natural splendour and infect you with a sort of reggae-induced repose, is not a place where it pays to be careless. So, while the beaches may look inviting, think twice before swimming in the marked sections as even an expert would do well to overcome the area's notoriously powerful riptides.

As regards when to come, well, if a large part of your motivation is to escape from the misery of home climes, then you'd do well to avoid the rainy seasons, which run from May to June and September to November each year. Outside of these months, expect the mercury to register a fairly satisfying 25 to 30 degrees, with no shortage of sunshine. But irrespective of when you travel - rainy season or dry — be aware that you will have to pay for the pleasure of your visit — roughly £12 each time you pass through the entrance-gate. Also worth remembering is that refreshment prices inside the park do not correlate with those in the rest of the area, so visitors would be well-advised to stock up on essentials before they go inside and carry them with them.

But, forgetting the riptides and inflated prices, in the final analysis what Tayrona National Parks has to offer is rather special and unique. You will not have hordes of noisy tourists following in your wake and trampling over your dreams of peace and tranquillity; this is the road less travelled, and it rewards those intrepid and adventurous types who go the extra mile in search of something real in spades. Tayrona is unspoilt; her wildlife precious; her beaches sublime, and, for those who respect and appreciate her, a once-in-a-lifetime experience awaits. Take the road less travelled; hike her forest paths; camp in her belly; lay on her golden beaches; listen to her wild music — do so and you simply cannot fail to be inspired.

31. **Tayrona National Park**

A. is known more for the quality of its beaches than it is for the diversity of its wildlife.

B. is equally well-known for its beaches and the variety of wildlife which inhabits the area.

C. has a number of excellent beaches dotted along its coast which are home to a huge variety of wildlife.

D. is being developed in the hope that it will one day earn a reputation as a tourist hotspot.

32. **What does the writer say about getting to the park?**

A. taking a taxi will cost you a lot of money

B. it is inadvisable to hire a car for the journey as the models available are not adequate

C. the journey by bus from Santa Marta to Tayrona lasts 30 minutes

D. a bus from the region's capital will take you no further than the park entrance

33. **What does the writer imply in the third paragraph?**

A. the park interior may officially be called a conservation area but it is not really treated like one

B. you will need to spend more than the typical number of days on holiday here to get the most out of it

C. all visitors to the park have to travel in by day and leave before nightfall

D. there are a number of posh hotels within the confines of the park itself

34. **The Arrecifes area**

A. is a very charming place, full of natural beauty, that will make you feel calm inside.

B. is a coastal site with a number of safe and inviting beaches which are used by many swimmers.

C. as a whole is really not suitable for swimming in even if you are an expert swimmer.

D. is a place with which there is a very strong association with reggae music.

35. **The writer suggests that**

A. refreshments are cheaper to buy inside the park .

B. refreshment prices within the park are little different to those in the surrounding area.

C. a one-off payment of approximately £12 is required to secure a pass that enables you to use the entrance gate freely.

D. you will save money by bringing refreshments into the park with you.

36. **Which of the following statements best sums up the writer's view of the experience of visiting the park?**

A. for those who put in a little extra effort, they will find the visit very rewarding

B. visitors to the park in general will find it an inspiring experience

C. it is possible to escape from the noisy, touristy parts of the park and find a quite area of peace and tranquility but this requires some extra effort

D. you have to travel for an extra mile further inside the park in order to escape the crowds of noisy tourists

PART 6   Reading   **Questions 37-43**

You are going to read an extract from a magazine article. Seven paragraphs have been removed from the extract. Choose from the paragraphs A-H the one which fits each gap (37-43). There is one extra paragraph you do not need to use. Mark your answers on the separate answer sheet.

Threading a Fine Line

Monica Carmody profiles Mario Balotelli, an athlete quite capable of the sublime, but also occasionally prone to the ridiculous.

The beginnings of his professional career were played out by Balotelli at Lumezzane in the 2005/2006 season. Often subjected to racist taunts and provocation from fans of the opposing teams, this did little to stem the emerging volatility in his character; a temperamental Balotelli was soon known as much for his explosive outbursts and often times odd behaviour off the pitch as he was for his prolific talent on. But despite his capriciousness and penchant for the bizarre, the Italian giant, Inter Milan, was prepared to roll the dice and take a chance on him, banking on that prodigious talent more than compensating for probable off-field shenanigans and devilment.

37

It wasn't long before Mancini was back in football however, and, with Mourinho and Balotelli frequently clashing both on and off the field, the possibility of a reunion, first sounded out by representatives of the owners of Manchester City (Mancini's new club) during the latter half of the 2009-2010 season, seemed more and more likely. In the end, Balotelli had little option but to look towards pastures new; not only had his manager grown tired of his antics, but so too, it seemed, had the fans, a number of whom even got into a physical confrontation with him after a match; so much had feelings between them and the player disintegrated.

38

That Balotelli was a loose cannon was never denied by Mancini, who is quoted as saying, 'He's crazy – but I love him because he's a good guy'. Besides, loose cannons, while capable of inflicting minor injuries on those fuelling them, also have the capacity, if properly deployed, to deliver a terminal blow to the opposition – so long as the PR damage Balotelli caused to his club was more than compensated for by his exploits with the football, neither Mancini nor the Board of Directors of Manchester City Football Club would have too many qualms about keeping him on their books.

39

This much is clear when it comes to Balotelli; he has an aura about him that few footballers, past or present, have ever had. He is magnetic and when he walks into a room, he soon has its occupants rapt; there is something endearing about his unrefined persona. And perhaps this is what attracts young people to him. Mario Balotelli leaves it all out there; he is an open book, but not one which will gather dust on the coffee table for weeks; his is the kind the pages of which you cannot stop turning once you've begun to read.

40

Their loyalty aside though, serious doubts remain about whether Balotelli will be the author of his own great destiny, or whether he is penning a tale of self-inflicted doom. His club has just won an historic league championship for the first time in a generation, and the Italian national team in which he featured prominently also gave an excellent account of itself on the European stage, beating the mighty Germans 2-0, courtesy of two Balotelli specials, before falling at the final hurdle to the Spanish, who, as a team collective, are arguably the greatest unit European football has ever produced. There can be no doubt about it; for now, at least, Balotelli is riding high and his stock is on the up and up.

41

It is, in many respects, refreshing to see a player in the glare of the media so confidently cast off the veil of machismo that so many of his peers permanently wear and hide behind, and it makes it, perhaps, all the easier to empathise with the man when we see this vulnerable, emotional, human side to him. This type of behaviour only cements his place in the hearts of fans and wins him new ones.

42

Silvia nursed him back to health and although Mario remained in contact with his birth siblings, Abigail, Enoch and Angel, he became estranged from his real parents, never, it seems, able to bring himself to forgive them for giving him up. Aged 11, when he first signed for Lumezzane, Mario refused to play under the Barwuah name. Seven years on, he obtained his Italian citizenship, flanked by Silvia and her husband, Francesco. The first the Barwuahs heard about this was when an article appeared in a local newspaper the next day.

43

Nevertheless, however much we can empathise with the little boy hurt, and his tomfoolery, he remains somewhat of a liability as long as it continues, and how those unwritten chapters will read is far from clear. At only 21, he has, really, his whole life ahead of him, and the world is his proverbial oyster. His friends and family must hope that his antics will mellow in time.

A

But unlike Milan's blind gamble, Mancini's City was taking a calculated one. After all, Mancini already knew what would be coming his way, and, more importantly, he had handled, or, at least, tolerated, the player's indiscretions before. He was realistic enough not to expect the circus show to end just like that, but he did expect its star clown to save his best performances for on the pitch and not to do anything too radical or detrimental off.

B

Just how much this newfound success meant to him on a personal level was plain to see in his behaviour post-match after the game against Germany. When the final whistle blew, Balotelli ran to the side of the pitch, there to be greeted by a mother beaming with pride. The two embraced in a scene few could fail to be moved by, and Balotelli, clearly elated as he spoke to television crews from across Europe minutes later, went on to dedicate his performance on the night to his mum Silvia.

C

As things turned out, they needn't have been too concerned anyway. The Balotelli of the north-England side was a new beast, as breathtakingly brilliant and precocious as ever when he donned the team jersey, but far more docile than before in his other private and public forays. Indeed, the fans took him to their hearts at once and he developed somewhat of a cult following among the City faithful. 'All the kids want to be him', commented one local football correspondent – perhaps a slightly worrying if accurate appraisal!

D

It was after this transfer that Balotelli became acquainted with Robert Mancini for the first time, while the latter was still heading things up at the club prior to his unceremonious sacking in May 2008. The two formed an unlikely bond, Mancini identifying a goodness of character in the eccentric and unpredictable Balotelli which he came to admire. But their football relationship was brought to an end prematurely with the announcement that the cocky little Portuguese manager, Mourinho, was to replace Mancini – a first blot on the latter's otherwise immaculate managerial record.

E

In theory, much of this story has yet to be written and his career at City is only the first of many new chapters that should see him grow and mature into a great club and international striker, and a sporting superstar, but with Balotelli only one thing is assured; the road will be a bumpy one and there will be lots of twists and turns along the way. Meanwhile, his fans will continue to turn the pages as they are written, and Balotelli can rest assured that, whatever happens, his readership won't abandon him at least.

F

But, delve deeper, beyond this fleeting show of emotion, and you discover the real story of Mario Balotelli, and, if empathy is your thing, then it doesn't get much more evocative than this… For a start you may have noticed (it is hard not to) that Mario and Silvia are not of the same ethnicity. The contrast between them is stark; she is a pale-faced Italian and he has the very dark complexion one would if they were of Ghanaian descent. In fact, Silvia is his foster mum, with whom he lived from the age of three onwards when social services took him away from his birth parents, Thomas and Rose Barwuah, on account of their cramped living conditions, which were not suitable for a child such as Mario, suffering from a life-threatening intestinal condition.

G

Other accounts of his unpredictability are far more endearing, though Balotelli himself has denied they ever occurred. One such case is the story of a homeless man Balotelli presented with £1,000, exclaiming, according to the recipient of the gift, that he liked his ginger dreadlocks. On another occasion, while signing autographs, he was introduced to a child who had been bullied at school. He is then alleged to have accompanied the child to his school grounds to confront the bullies. Imagine what they must have been thinking to themselves as big Mario came towards them!

H

Some psychologists believe that Mario, scarred by his early-life experiences, behaves eccentrically to draw attention to himself in a superficial kind of way; to give journalists the ammunition they need to write their stories without having to delve deeper into his background and personal life. The bravado and clowning around, they say, is probably just a smokescreen. In any case, given the physical powerhouse the man has become, his desire to forget a weak and vulnerable childhood, if it is that, is entirely understandable. And perhaps he lives life on the wild side today simply by virtue of the fact that he can, something that was not always guaranteed while he was growing up. Or perhaps his roguishness is his way of making the most of life, Balotelli being, one can imagine, far more appreciative of what he has than are most of his footballing peers.

CPE Practice Test 5

You are going to read an article about great tennis players. For questions 44-53, choose from the people (A-E). The people may be chosen more than once. Mark your answers on the separate answer sheet.

To which person does each statement relate?

He was determined to make a transition that required him to come out of his comfort zone and alter his style of play. **44** [ ]

Impeding him in his quest to succeed is a type of pressure over which he has no control that most other players are unaccustomed to. **45** [ ]

Despite enjoying a hot streak of form during which he landed some major titles, he has yet to convince the tennis world of his greatness. **46** [ ]

He pushes himself physically to such a degree that his career may be cut short. **47** [ ]

He took excellent advantage of a temporary lack of depth in his sport. **48** [ ]

He was faced with the task of having to try to overcome seasoned champions in title matches in his efforts to claim a first Grand Slam. **49** [ ]

He has an attribute which is both an advantage he can use to devastating effect, as well as a potential handicap. **50** [ ]

He has a history of health issues, which may jeopardise both his longevity and legacy. **51** [ ]

He endured an unusually long period out of the winner's enclosure at one point in his career. **52** [ ]

He dominated a rival for a season only to later taste defeat in a title-decider at the hands of the same player. **53** [ ]

The Era of Greatness

It is rare enough even for two greats to have careers which coincide and see them pitted against one another on a regular basis, so for there to be so many giants all competing on court at the same time at the peak of their powers, as is the case today, is well, quite simply remarkable.

ROGER FEDERER   A

Roger Federer is the man who, on paper at least, is the undisputed greatest of them all. He has smashed virtually every record in existence and amassed an incredible seventeen Grand Slam titles, a full three more than his nearest rival, Pete Sampras. On court, he is a sight to behold; barely ever breaking into a sweat and making his every shot seem completely effortless. What's more, the Swiss star radiates calmness and never, outwardly at least, seems to get ruffled. Now 30, he has had a pretty barren spell by his lofty standards of late, but did manage to break a two-year major-title drought at Wimbledon, in 2012, beating Andy Murray in the final. On the strength of his record, he could be regarded as the greatest player by some margin, but, title tally aside, there are other things to consider here, such as the fact that his rise to prominence coincided with a time of transition in the sport when the existing powers – Sampras, Agassi etc. – were on the wane and ready to pass on the baton to a new generation. Federer was a very willing recipient of course, but, truth told, he beat a lot of second-rate players and players past their prime in the process of amassing over half his total haul of slams in those early years. But, with the emergence of Nadal, that would all change. In Nadal, Federer was given a true test, and one in which the great man came up short. Their head-to-head in CPE last five years is very one-sided in Nadal's favour, and the Spaniard has been utterly dominant in the high-stakes matches they have played. Indeed, while no one can question Federer's God-given talent, Nadal exposed an aspect of his game which is very suspect; his ability to perform under pressure on the big stage and in the big points when it mattered. The emergence of Novak Djokovic has only led to Federer's successes becoming even more infrequent, and his failure to overcome Nadal and Djokovic, his greatest tests, has left question marks over his legacy. His Wimbledon comeback of 2012 has gone a way towards redemption, but, that said, he didn't have to overcome his arch nemesis, Nadal, so the jury is still out.

Rafael Nadal

Nadal, like most Spaniards, grew up playing on clay. It is hardly surprising then, that his playing style is best-suited to the surface, nor that he favoured the red soil in those early days and produced his best performances on it, while, at the same time, struggling initially to make any impact on grass or hard courts. His compatriots had the same difficulties, and some even boycotted the entire grass-court season, such was their disdain for the surface. But not Nadal, who was unafraid of trying to learn and improve his game, and who was keen to reinvent himself as an all-rounder. Before long, he was the undisputed king of clay, but few people gave him much hope of success elsewhere. His reinvention, however, must surely have surpassed the expectations of even his most optimistic and faithful supporters, for adapt his game he did, and so successfully that by 2008 he was ready to do the unthinkable, beating a peak-of-his-powers Federer on his favourite surface, grass, in the Wimbledon final, sending shockwaves through the sport. The pundits were soon contemplating, 'if he can beat the Fed on grass, what else is he capable of?' Their answer came soon enough as Nadal went on to dominate men's tennis, and his arch rival Federer, for the best part of the next three years, beating him in every slam final in which they met one another. To the world of tennis, it was suddenly clear that, whatever it said on paper, Nadal was the stronger of the two men. While no one could compete with Federer in the talent stakes, Nadal showed himself to be a superior match player and fighter; he knew how to close out under pressure better than anyone. His legacy, therefore, seemed assured, but there was one man who had other ideas and who fancied a shot at greatness himself. Cue Novac Djokovic, who, in 2011, showed Nadal how it feels to be utterly dominated on court. Nadal's comeback has already begun, however, and, unlike Federer, he has managed to beat his nemesis in a slam final again since tasting defeat. But it remains to be seen if his career can have the longevity of the Fed's, so demanding is his style of play on the body.

Novak Djokovic

And so we move on to the Serb, a player who it seemed for all too long would have to be satisfied with playing second fiddle to Federer and Nadal, and collecting the odd trophy here and there when, for one reason or another, fortune had conspired to send both of his arch rivals on their way out of a tournament. But then along came 2011, which, for Novak Djokovic, was truly a watershed year. At last he prevailed over the previously invincible Nadal, and not in one slam final but three. Suddenly, tennis had a new number one. Djokovic had transformed himself into the most consistent, hard-hitting, counter-attacking player on the circuit — a title he had prised away from Nadal. 2012 also started well for the new poster boy of tennis, but Djokovic's level has since dropped considerably, and both Nadal and Federer have enjoyed success over him in their recent tussles. Therefore, while it looked, momentarily at least, as if Djokovic would conquer all before him and cement his place as one of if not the best player in history, much remains for him to prove yet. Otherwise, 2011 will be viewed as an anomaly, a sort of accident of sport which saw him play above his level for an unusually lengthy period. But only the passage of time will reveal if that was indeed the case.

Andy Murray

By comparison to the achievements of the players already profiled, Murray's record looks pretty ordinary, and yet, were it not for the fact that he has had the misfortunate to play the game at the same time as arguably the three greatest sportsmen to have ever graced the court, this talented all-rounder would already have amassed a stash of major trophies of his own. As things stand however, despite showing much promise, he has yet to capture any of the four coveted slams, and, though tantalising close, is thus far just shy of the level his arch rivals have reached and needs to raise his game if he is to stand a chance of emulating their achievements. The cross he has to bear, though, is unlike anything that they are faced with, for Murray, ever since he showed glimpses of brilliance as a youth on his way to winning the U.S. Open at underage level, has had the weight of expectation of an entire nation pressing on his young shoulders, encumbering his every move on court. And besides, unlike Federrer, Nadal and Djokovic, who faced debutants when winning their first grand slams, Murray has had no such luck, and, rather than encountering first-timers, has, in fact, on every occasion he has made it to the last two, faced the daunting prospect of having to overcome one of the aforementioned trio.

Jo-Wilfried Tsonga

On his day, he is a match for any player, a fact he has proved on more than one occasion, most notably in his comeback from two sets to love down against Federer in the 2011 Wimbledon Quarterfinal. Capable of generating electrifying pace and hitting hot streaks that make him virtually unplayable, Tsonga is a crowd favourite wherever he goes simply because he is pure theatre; when he walks out on court, either something magical will happen or there will be an epic fail. That he can compete with the best is beyond question, but the Frenchman has yet to string together a consistent run of performances, something which he must learn to do if he is to become a genuine slam contender and fulfil the promise he has shown. He has come on in leaps and bounds over the last year or two though, and the only thing that may hold him back in the future is his large, muscular frame, which, though advantageous in the sense that it fuels his outrageous hitting power, has also proved a barrier to progress on account of it making him very susceptible to injury. Indeed, injury has plagued Tsonga since the early days of his career and his greatest challenge, if he is to go on to one day bag a slam, may prove to be that of overcoming his own bodily frailties.

Writing

PART 1 Writing   Question 1

Read the two texts below.

Write an essay summarising and evaluating the key points from both texts. Use your own words throughout as far as possible, and include your own ideas in your answers.

Write your answer in **240-280** words.

1.

Sport – vital for fostering life skills

Experience in the sporting arena is as important to a young person's development as is their formal education. Participation in sport teaches young people vital life skills including mechanisms for dealing with success and failure. It also fosters a sense of team spirit and cooperation, without which young people would struggle to succeed and reach their full potential in later life. Sport, on account of its competitive nature, also teaches athletes that little in life is gained except through hard work, as well as the importance of being prepared to compete with your rivals in order to achieve your goals.

A Nation of Layabouts

The obesity epidemic that is sweeping the nation is only symptomatic of the sedentary nature of modern living. How do we expect to stay in shape when we abandon all physical pursuit for the living room sofa, on which we are masters of little more than the T.V. remote control and the computer mouse. Unless young people are encouraged to venture into the outdoors and to get active again, the problem will only be worse in a decade or so's time when the new generation has reached maturity. But in a world where parents are as guilty of slouching around as their children, where are we going to find the role models to show them the way?

Write your **essay**.

PART 2 Writing   **Questions 2-4**

Write an answer to **one** of the questions **2-4** in this part. Write your answer in **280-320** words in an appropriate style on the separate answer sheet. Put the question number in the box at the top of the answer sheet.

2. An entertainment magazine is running a series of reviews of films that tackle serious themes to do with growing up, and which would be of educational benefit to young people today. You decide to send in a review in which you describe a film about coping with being a teenager, mentioning what problems of adolescence the film highlights and why you would recommend it to a young audience.

Write your **review**.

3. A science magazine is running a series of articles on inventions and discoveries which have revolutionised the way we live. The magazine has invited readers to send in articles briefly describing the invention or discovery they regard as having been most significant, explaining the ways in which this invention or discovery has impacted our day-to-day lives and why they regard it as more important than other inventions and discoveries that have been made.

Write your **article**.

4. A study-abroad fair was recently held in your town for international educational institutes to promote their courses and study programmes. You have been asked to write a report on the study-abroad fair for your school website. You should briefly describe the event and identify two or three ways in which students who want to study abroad but who are constrained by money issues can achieve their goal. You should also evaluate the extent to which such events can adequately inform young people about the range of study-abroad options available and the potential problems students who study abroad should be prepared to face.

Write your **report**.

Listening

You will hear three different extracts. For questions 1-6, choose the answer (A, B, or C) which fits best according to what you hear. There are two questions for each extract.

EXTRACT 1

You hear a lecturer is psychology talking about the Western World's attitude to Dubai.

1. What transformation has Dubai made?
    A. it has turned into a global centre of trade
    B. it has moved away from a consumerist mentality
    C. it has become a major tourism hub

2. What does the speaker find disturbing?
    A. the way tourists embrace Dubai's capitalist culture
    B. tourists' willingness to pretend not to see the injustices going on
    C. tourists' ignorance about what is really happening

EXTRACT 2

You hear two guests on a radio talk show discussing a recent banking scandal.

3. What did the report reveal?
    A. U.K. and U.S. banks were laundering money
    B. widespread misconduct in the U.K. banking system
    C. an isolated case of improper conduct by a U.K. bank

4. What does the female speaker think should happen to those in charge of the banks?
    A. they should be forced to quit their jobs
    B. they should have to stand trial
    C. they should admit their guilt and move on

EXTRACT 3

You hear a lecturer in politics talking to a group of students about tactics in U.S. presidential elections.

5. What point is the speaker making about Kennedy's choice of running mate?
    A. it was a confusing one since the two men were not likeminded
    B. it is preferable to pick a running mate with contrasting political views
    C. his decision was motivated by wanting to win; not personality

6. Why did John McCain fall out of favour with the public?
    A. he was a poor public speaker
    B. his running mate undermined his credibility
    C. he was associated with incompetence and corruption

PART 2   Listening   Questions 7-15

You will hear a journalist talking about the life of a famous Scottish poet.
For questions 7-15 complete the sentences with a word or short phrase.

Thanks to his parents' advocacy, Burns dedicated himself fully to his [7 _____]

and developed a love of reading.

Burns found a release for his frustration at his impoverishment by turning to drink and taking a keen

interest in members of [8 _____] .

The fathering of children out of wedlock caused a [9 _____] for the

Burns' and Armour's families.

Burns' first book of verse enjoyed [10 _____], a factor which motivated

him to remain in his homeland.

In Edinburgh, Burns mingled in [11 _____] and made some very wealthy

and important friends.

Burns' [12 _____] became more extreme over time, and he started to

use his writings as a means to express them.

His [13 _____] was part of the reason for the rapid deterioration of his

health, as was his early-years toil.

The day he was laid to rest coincided with that of the [14 _____] of one

of his sons.

Burns has a considerable number of living [15 _____], a legacy of having

fathered 12 children during his life.

PART 3 Listening Questions 16-20

You will hear part of a discussion between two well-known business people, Sam Boland and Jimmy Glynn, and a radio current affairs show host about a recent newspaper article on the subject of jobless graduates. For questions 16-20, choose the answer (A, B, C or D) which first best according to what you hear.

16 What does Jimmy say about the qualifications graduate jobseekers have?
   A. they help them avoid having to take 'survival jobs'
   B. few graduates are sufficiently qualified for the jobs available
   C. few degrees teach skills relevant in the workplace
   D. they are not really an advantage in the present job market

17 Why is Sam wary of employing graduates in his own company?
   A. their superior performance can lead to workplace hostility
   B. they can have a damaging effect on the chemistry of their team
   C. he prefers to hire unskilled workers and invest in training
   D. they only accept positions above lesser-skilled employees

18 In what respect have things changed since the speakers were job-seeking graduates?
   A. jobseekers used not to lie about their qualifications
   B. jobseekers used to pretend they had better qualifications
   C. jobseekers used to be far fresher and more enthusiastic
   D. jobseekers used not to mind dumbing down their CVs

19 Why does Jimmy have some sympathy for graduates?
   A. he admires their sense of entitlement
   B. they were too young to understand what they voted for
   C. they have accumulated huge debts ul college
   D. they are victims of other people's incompetence

20 Jimmy believes that college-goers of the future should
   A. not rule out the Arts and Humanities.
   B. work for foreign in preference to local firms.
   C. choose their courses of study carefully.
   D. be selective about where they study.

PART 4 Listening Questions 21-30

You will hear five short extracts in which athletes talk about how they got into their sports and what they put their success down to. You will hear the recording twice. While you listen, you must complete both tasks.

TASK ONE

For questions 21-25, choose from the list (A-H) how each athlete became interested in their sport.

A	they discovered it on vacation abroad	Speaker 1 — 21
B	they did it as a way to deal with a drug and alcohol problem	
C	they saw it as a chance to impress a love interest	Speaker 2 — 22
D	they had a very competitive and motivational parent	
E	they wanted to emulate their parent	Speaker 3 — 23
F	their parents were thrill-seekers	
G	it was a way to keep them occupied	Speaker 4 — 24
H	it is a sport they associate with their national identity	Speaker 5 — 25

TASK TWO

For questions 26-30, choose from the list (A-H) what each athlete says is behind their success.

A	hard work and commitment	Speaker 1 — 26
B	mental strength and positive thinking	
C	a passion shared with a colleague	Speaker 2 — 27
D	a desire to make the most of their talents	
E	a strong cultural association with their sport	Speaker 3 — 28
F	a desire to become more disciplined	
G	a desire to compete against others	Speaker 4 — 29
H	the continuing search for love	Speaker 5 — 30

Test 6

Reading

PART 1   Reading   **Questions 1-8**

For questions 1-8, read the text below and decide which answer (A, B, C or D) best fits each gap. Mark your answers on the separate answer sheet. There is an example at the beginning (0).

Example   **0 A** synonymous   **B** familiar   **C** representative   **D** connected

Higgs Boson

July 4th is fairly (0).......... with the celebration of American independence. However, it is also now the day on which an announcement of (1).......... significance was made by scientists at CERN, whose work at the Large Hadron Collider has finally (2).......... statistically significant proof of the existence of the Higgs Boson – the particle that represents the missing (3).......... in the puzzle that is how our universe (4).......... into being.

What was once an exclusive conversation piece of those heavily (5).......... in particle physics, the Higgs Boson became hot (6).......... talk following the release of a series of Hollywood movies based loosely around the discovery of a so-called 'God Particle', which, without wanting to be too crude about it, the Higgs Boson basically is.

The announcement, therefore, received widespread media coverage and has been (7).......... as possibly the most significant scientific breakthrough of our time. Arguably, it brings a(n) (8).......... to the long-running debate about how the universe began.

1.	A	ornamental	B	monumental	C	outstanding	D	memorable
2.	A	earned	B	accrued	C	permitted	D	yielded
3.	A	slice	B	piece	C	fraction	D	share
4.	A	went	B	moved	C	sprang	D	drifted
5.	A	engrossed	B	participated	C	involved	D	included
6.	A	common	B	topic	C	table	D	subject
7.	A	adopted	B	hinted	C	honoured	D	hailed
8.	A	ultimatum	B	end	C	limit	D	terminal

PART 2   Reading   **Questions 9-16**

For questions 9-16 read the text below and think of the word which best fits each gap. Use only one word in each space. There is an example at the beginning (0).

Example: **0**   A T

Greatness

It is rare indeed that we have the opportunity to behold **(0)**......**at**..... work the titanic forces that prime the Earth's massifs, those monumental ranges that are the **(9)**................................. of legend; that represent the pinnacle of human conquest; that tease mankind and dare it to attempt a summit climb, **(10)**................................. the treachery and deadliness of the path that leads to dizzying success and immortality. Many have started the quest and failed, some **(11)**................................. the ultimate price, and it is not **(12)**................................. our mountaineers and explorers who seek to surmount the insurmountable; humanity as a **(13)**................................. has, forever it seems, had a morbid sort of fascination with nature's tallest, indelibly snow-capped peaks. **(14)**................................. is it only the prospect of their ascent that piques the interest; it is their very existence; we gaze up at them from the depths of normality — from the pitiful elevations of ground level — and all of us, in our own way, dream of becoming master of their heights and of viewing the world from atop their menacing crests. The photographer captures his dream in that perfect image, content to idealise the prospect of the ultimate challenge — it is for others to master, not him. The writer translates his dreams into prose, romanticising the quest, compelling other **(15)**................................. courageous souls to take those first brave steps into the unknown, whence they may never return, save in lore. The journalist reports their successes and failures with equal measures of gusto — for him, the story ends well **(15)**................................. way.

PART 3   Reading   **Questions 17-24**

For questions 17-24, read the text below. Use the word given in capitals at the end of the lines to form a word that fits in the space in the same line. There is an example at the beginning (0).
Write your answers **IN CAPITAL LETTERS** on the separate answer sheet.

Example: **0**   p r e t e n c e

Breaking the Laws of Attraction

A new study has revealed that the mere **(0)** _**pretence**_ of attraction, provided it is backed up by a   PRETEND
conscious **(17)**................................. to become attracted can turn into a self-fulfilling prophesy.   CONVINCE

In a speed-dating experiment, **(18)**................................. were asked to play **(19)**................................. games   PART/PSYCHE
designed to encourage attraction, including looking into each other's eyes, sharing secrets and gift-giving.

In conventional speed-dating sessions fewer than one in five men or women typically express a desire
to see any of their dating partners again. However, the psychological games appeared to increase the
success rate **(20)**................................. , with almost 45% of males or females providing positive feedback   SUBSTANCE
about at least one of their dates.

The **(21)**................................. scientists conducting the experiment concluded that in much the same way   BEHAVE
as forcing yourself to smile can actually increase **(22)**................................., pairs of people behaving as if   HAPPY
they find one another **(23)**................................. can convince themselves that they do.   ATTRACT

Taken to the extreme, the technique could, in principle, be used to **(24)**................................. two complete   ABLE
strangers to fall madly in love.

For questions 25-30, complete the second sentence so that it has a similar meaning to the first sentence, using the word given. Do not change the word given. You must use between three and eight words, including the word given. Here is an example (0).

Example:

0   I think I just saw Frankie for a split second driving past in a Ferrari no less.   caught

     I think I just .... for a split second driving past in a Ferrari no less.

Write only the missing words on the separate answer sheet. | 0 | caught sight of Frankie |

25. No matter what happens, we will never make the same mistake again.

    ever

    Under .... the same mistake again.

26. Eleanor concluded that the whole idea had been a mistake.

    came

    Eleanor .... the whole idea had been a mistake.

27. Jane certainly wasn't going to accept Alex's apology last night.

    mood

    Jane .... from Alex last night.

28. The news of her sudden death came as a great shock to all the mayor's relatives and friends.

    aback

    The mayor's relatives and friends .... sudden death.

29. Jane didn't get the job because she wasn't experienced enough.

    down

    Jane's .... lack of experience.

30. The project was not cleared to begin until a full planning appeal had been heard.

    hearing

    Only .... the project finally cleared to begin.

PART 5 Reading | **Questions 31-36**

You are going to read an article about a new technology used to authenticate paintings. For questions 31-36, choose the answer (A, B, C or D) which you think fits best according to the text. Mark your answers on the separate answer sheet.

Science Forces Rethink on Rubens Masterpiece

The so-called experts, the most esteemed minds of the art world, were both adamant and unanimous in their insistence that The Young Anthony was a Rubens masterpiece, but now, it seems, technology has proven them all wrong in their assertions, with an X-ray study of the painting confirming it as a self-portrait of Sir Anthony Van Dyck. The Rubens connection is still there, of course – Van Dyck being a former student of his who went on to serve as court painter to Charles I of England – but this will be scant consolation for the critics who have espoused for so long the notion that only Rubens could have produced such a work. For them, embarrassment and a large serving of humble pie await, and rightly so given their frequently petulant dismissal and intolerance of those who hold views contrary to their own. The way they behave, it is as though to question them is to commit some form of heinous crime. How can the mighty art experts be wrong? Well, perhaps this dose of humiliation is a timely reminder to them that we are all fallible and that their assumption of superiority on all matters art-related – an elitist, self-serving attitude – is entirely bogus.

The technology employed to reveal the secrets of this particular masterpiece is being used more and more now to analyse the works of world-renowned artists. In one recent case, a new Rembrandt piece, Old Man with a Beard, was discovered. Critics had long dismissed this painting as a crude imitation by one of his students. Cue another large portion of humble pie... But they do not always get it completely wrong, as an examination of Still Life with Meadow Flowers and Roses revealed. The authenticity of this piece as a genuine Van Gogh had long been disputed, but the X-ray analysis confirmed what the vast majority of critics had believed for years. Another fascinating aspect of that particular study was the discovery of the fact that Van Gogh had painted his masterpiece atop another of his works featuring a depiction of two half-naked wrestlers, a painting he had described in letters but which was presumed destroyed.

What gave away the identity of Sir Anthony as the painter of The Young Anthony also had to do with the discovery of a painted-over image on the canvas. Apparently, this particular underpainting was very similar in style and technique to a number of Sir Anthony's other works, leaving experts in no doubt as to the creatorship of the over-painted portrait which sat on top of it. And the discovery, though surely an embarrassment for the Rubens House Museum in Antwerp, where The Young Anthony is housed, has a silver lining of sorts; Rubens was rather a prolific painter of self-portraits, so despite his name being attached to The Young Anthony, its value was estimated to be only about €1 million - a mere trifle for a Rubens - on account of the relative abundance of such pieces. On the other hand, as the work of Sir Anthony, its value could rise considerably – as much as double – by virtue of the fact that he was not nearly as prolific as Rubens when it came to this form of art.

As to the technology to which we owe this discovery, Synchrotron radiation, it was initially regarded by scientists as little more than a nuisance, and only came to their attention because it was the cause of energy being drained from the first particle accelerators (precursors of The Large Hadron Collider physicists at CERN used to discover the elusive Higgs Boson). Scientists trying to understand their machines' failure to produce the level of energy intensity required to smash particles such as electrons together found that much of the energy generated was being converted into X-rays (Synchrotron radiation) and effectively being lost. To fix the problem, expensive radiation shielding had to be put up. But despite its rather inglorious and bothersome introduction, on further study, scientists soon came to see Synchrotron radiation in itself as a powerful tool for studying the properties of matter. Today, this type of radiation is used extensively in the analysis of the elemental composition of material and the chemical state of said elements. It can provide data accurate at microscopic levels of analysis, which is what makes it so useful for the inspection of works of art. And, as well as being used to authenticate works, Synchrotron radiation also has a role to play in conserving the world's masterpieces for generations to come, by helping us to understand the reasons why and manner in which some paints fade or change their characteristics over time.

31. **What does the writer say about the painting The Young Anthony?**

A. whether or not Rubens is its creator is still a hotly contested point in art circles

B. new technology revealed that it is a Rubens masterpiece which contradicts an assertion made by art experts

C. it is a source of humiliation for so-called art experts who originally credited it to the wrong artist

D. an X-ray study confirmed its authenticity as a self-portrait of Sir Anthony Van Dyck, something critics had long suspected

32. **Old Man with a Beard**

A. is a painting which, following X-ray analysis, has been confirmed as the work of a student of Rembrandt's.

B. is another piece for which an X-ray analysis has contradicted the views of critics.

C. has been exposed as a crude imitation of a Rembrandt through X-ray analysis.

D. is a painting for which the X-ray analysis confirmed the existing doubts critics had.

33. **The writer uses the example of Still Life with Meadow Flowers and Roses**

A. to show that critics are not always wrong in their assertions.

B. to highlight the fact that the authenticity of some Van Gogh works is also in question.

C. as it was only recently identified as an underpainting.

D. to show how lost paintings can be recovered and put back on display thanks to X-ray technology.

34. **What is true of the self-portrait The Young Anthony?**

A. its value has been reduced as a result of the findings of the X-ray study

B. it has now been confirmed as a rare piece whose value is likely to rise

C. as a Rubens piece it was worth as much as twice the amount it can now command

D. originally, it was an underpainting but it has since been restored and is now on display in the Rubens House Museum

35. Synchrotron radiation

A. was originally employed by scientists to stop energy being drained from the first particle accelerators.

B. was discovered by scientists when they identified it as the cause of energy loss from the first particle accelerators.

C. is a form of expensive radiation shielding put up in order to prevent energy leakage from particle accelerators.

D. is regarded for the most part by scientists as a fairly unexceptional and annoying form of radiation that does little other than cause a nuisance during experiments in particle physics.

36. **Which of the following statements is true based on the information in the passage?**

A. The writer appears to have a lot of respect for art critics, whose opinions he seems to value highly.

B. The writer suggests that Synchrotron radiation has a usefulness to the art world that extends beyond the authentication of paintings.

C. The writer is keen to show up art critics, and, in his effort to do so, focuses on examples of their mistakes.

D. The writer believes that The Young Anthony, when originally thought to be attributable to Rubens, was overvalued.

PART 6 Reading | **Questions 37-43**

You are going to read a short story. Seven paragraphs have been removed from the story. Choose from the paragraphs A-H the one which fits each gap (37-43). There is one extra paragraph you do not need to use. Mark your answers on the separate answer sheet.

The Laughing Stock of Centre Court

An extract from a short story by Finbarr Houghton

A British tennis player had not done well on tour for nearly a generation, so perhaps their desperation, their need to have someone to cheer for - some hope of glory - had led them to champion this plucky young Brit, who had walked out onto centre court wowing the crowd with his explosive play and dynamism, with a little too much fervour; perhaps they'd invested too much faith in this new kid on the block.

Then again, sure, it was only Round One, but when was the last time a British player had squared up to a top-tenner and even made a match of it, let alone emerged the other side of a five-set test of endurance the victor? It had been an amazing journey, now, looking back on it; Martin had played his way into the hearts and minds of the nation. First the Number 9 seed, then a qualifier; 'Okay', they must have thought, 'Round 3, we'll settle for that.'

37 _____

Indeed, the trepidation – what of it there was – was more inclined to be coming from the other side of the net, from a punch-drunk opponent hit with a tirade of outlandish winners – such was the story of Round 3. And soon, the hopes grew into a sense of expectation; after all, a nation reasoned, if he can play like this he can beat anyone. Well, his next opponent was not just anyone, he was a very definite someone; defending champion, in fact, and world number one; this would be the litmus test of Martin's nerves and whether he would buckle under the mounting pressure of shouldering the hopes of an expectant public demanding the end of the longest trophy drought in British tennis history.

38 _____

They would put the loss down as an anomaly; a freakish event that would not likely be repeated again for many moons. The Brits on the other hand were at last celebrating having got one over on those cocky Yanks, sick to the teeth of their patronising ways and having to watch them smirk as they walked away year after year with the coveted Wimbledon trophy, which, by rights, should have remained on home soil.

Now the nation had its champion-elect; destiny awaited, as did a quarter-final match and the prospect of having to play another top-tenner, the Number 5 seed, Max Kleinwort, the poster boy of German tennis. Well, Britain now had its own to cheer, so take that Max Kleinwort …

39 _____

It was not that they were cheering Martin the player as such at all, but only him as a means to an end, the end being the removal of the inferiority complex that had enveloped the entire nation. The newspaper scribes were already starting to write their eulogies, but you'd have done exceptionally well to decipher who they were supposed to be about. Martin's name was almost conspicuous by its absence. It was as though he had morphed into some new hero, dubbed British Tennis, and that this British Tennis fellow was playing in his stead for the remainder of the tournament.

40 _____

But his angst was well hidden, that much is sure. And the manner in which he dealt with it was, well, quite remarkable. Martin played like a veteran of ten last-eight matches, and anyone watching would have been excused for mistaking his opponent on the other side of the court for the debutant.

41 _____

But it was strange to behold his reaction – he gave nothing away; showed no emotion when he won – ever, in fact – and, this was starting to grate on some sections of his adoring public. They wanted their poster boy to have the charisma to go with his looks and talent; they wanted more. It would not be enough for Martin to win this title; he'd have to do it with style.

42 _____

Then, quietly and with little fuss, Martin stepped inside his home back into the real world; the world in which he went from being a glamorous tennis superstar to a helpless husband praying to God to grant him another day in the company of the only thing on the planet he had ever really loved or trusted; his dear beloved wife.

A weary Martin ushered his wife to the dining room sofa, then made his way to the kitchen to rustle up something they could have for dinner. Alice had not been to the shops today – a bad sign; she must have been hurting (the doctor couldn't increase her dosage of pain killers any higher without risking permanent damage to her health that would only accelerate her inevitable decline). But, if she was, she never let on to him. Cheese and bread; it would do.

43 _____

Another morning, and the dread of awakening came over Martin as usual; he quickly turned to his side and the relief on his face was palpable when his hand touched the warm skin of Alice's cheek; she was still here. He made her breakfast, with which she took her cocktail of medicines, before waving goodbye and going out to practise for the semi-final. Alice bade him farewell with a peck on the cheek, and that passing moment of affection was enough to steady Martin for whatever lay ahead.

A

But those with the knives out ready to write his obituary; ready to write off this petulant little Briton who had had the nerve to step out onto court and defy the formbook to cause a series of monumental upsets, had to put their blades away; Martin would make no hatchet job of this; another seed would fall, and it would be the biggest name of them all. George Sandeman was duly sent packing - scampering tail between legs back across the pond to his adoring Stateside public.

B

The ecstasy was reaching fever pitch as the morning of the match dawned. And yet, amid the furore of all this hype, no one seemed too bothered about getting to know their champion-in-waiting. Martin had kept his head low throughout, barely giving more than the mandatory clichéd few syllables in post-match press conferences. But the odd thing was, no one really cared what he had to say anyway.

C

It was hard, amid all the hype and the intensity, to remember that David Martin was just some ordinary Joe who had risen from oblivion to overnight stardom, cast as a near immortal, and who must surely have been quaking at the realisation of what his success was turning into – at the knowledge that the weight of expectation of an entire nation now rested on his shoulders. He was surely suffocating.

D

Martin put a plate of gorgonzola on toast on his wife's lap and returned moments later with his own meal. And, as had become their nightly ritual since the start of the tournament, he began to tell her all about his day. Alice, for her part, listened with the same intensity she always did when Martin spoke about his tennis; hearing of his success and sharing it with him privately was her one source of happiness now it seemed. She forgot the pain, momentarily at least, as she lost herself in the story retold. By the end of the tale, her fragile frame was glowing with pride and happiness. Martin smiled and reached out for her hand, and together they slowly drifted off into another world.

E

Martin had always hated tennis, truth told. It was his father who'd pushed him into the sport and he had always resented him for that. This was the first time he had had a reason to play for himself; seeing Alice take so much from his success had caused him to fall in love with the sport he had always despised; it had given him cause to unleash his considerable talents on his opponents at last. And now, for the first time, he wanted to win for himself – and, of course, for his beloved.

F

The atmosphere in the crowd was electric and perhaps this is what cowed the Number Five seed. It certainly emboldened Martin. He had this look of resoluteness and total calm in his eyes that must have sent shivers through the German poster boy as they shook hands before the match. Martin might just as well have had a walkover so one-sided was this affair.

G

But the story took on a life of its own and Martin played like a man possessed, and with the gung-ho attitude that surely only a carefree young upstart with nothing to lose can; there was no sense of fear in his eyes; no hint of it in his play.

H

That night, as David Martin opened the door to be met by his pale-faced, terminally ill childhood-sweetheart-come-wife Alice, it was clear that any reserves of pizzazz or panache or whatever you want to call it that he had were being saved for this moment; his expression changed in an instant and he sprang to life. The couple looked into one another's eyes a moment and then embraced. Just a big old simple hug, full of all the love an exhausted tennis-player husband and a wife on her third run of chemo can muster.

PART 7   Reading   Questions 44-53

You are going to read the transcript of a series of interviews with ordinary people conducted for the *Have your say* feature of a daily newspaper. For questions 44-53, choose from the people (A-D). The people may be chosen more than once.

Mark your answers on the separate answer sheet.

Which person gives each of these opinions about the education system?

The testing of very young people to determine their academic pedigree is unethical.

44 [ ]

The education system is designed in such a way as to unfairly favour people who have the money to invest in private education.

45 [ ]

Students in countries where extra evening classes have to be attended are more prone to feeling the effects of extreme tiredness.

46 [ ]

The policy of giving out higher grades is making a mockery of the entire testing system.

47 [ ]

The degree of difficulty of modern examinations is a lot lower than was the case for students sitting the same exams in the past.

48 [ ]

Children are more likely to engage with what they are learning if technology is incorporated into the teaching methods used.

49 [ ]

While our third level education system is well funded and very modern, we have neglected the primary level, where more investment is required.

50 [ ]

Students should not have to overly exert themselves study-wise in the evenings as they must also have the opportunity to enjoy their youth.

51 [ ]

While we are often quick to criticise the education system, most of us appreciate how fortunate we are in this country to have such a good one.

52 [ ]

Many capable people are prevented from pursuing a third level education due to the financial constraints they are under.

53 [ ]

Have your say ... on Education

Four ordinary different people give their views on the country's educational system.

Edward A

The British Education system is fundamentally flawed in numerous ways. For a start, I believe the 11-Plus exam is morally reprehensible. Children develop at different speeds, so to promote a situation where we divide up our young so early based on their performance in one stupid test seems to me ridiculous. Those who pass the 11-Plus are classed as success stories and they are expected to go on to do great things academically speaking in what essentially becomes a self-fulfilling prophesy. Meanwhile, at such a young age, those who don't manage to pass are already being labelled as failures and are told to set their sights low. This, sadly, also becomes a self-fulfilling prophesy - of the worst kind; if you expect to perform poorly and are of a mindset to do so, you will effectively underperform — it is as good as guaranteed. I see no reason why we have to set children up for a fall like this so early in life and divide them up into a two-tier education system which provides the upper tier with a massive advantage over the lower one. I mean, our society has enough class-based problems without manufacturing more. And that brings me to my next criticism. I believe the education system in this country is biased towards the privileged. Let's face it, the best education is the one which money can buy. Fee-paying schools consistently outperform schools in the state system, and only the wealthy can exploit the unfair advantage enjoyed by students who attend these exclusive institutions. And if that wasn't bad enough — as if ordinary working class people didn't face an uphill struggle already, if they do manage to make it through to university, they are then expected to pay astronomical fees. In many cases, they are simply priced out of a third-level education or are forced to take on a massive burden of debt to finance their studies. Meanwhile, mummy's little Eton boy can have his pick of universities and cost is no barrier. It is sad really just how unfair the whole system is.

Michelle C

I think our education system still commands a lot of respect and I think many other countries are still envious of the kinds of programmes we have in place, but I also worry that we are not investing enough money into schools to enable them to keep up with the latest classroom innovations. I mean, sure, our universities are state-of-the-art, but the formative years are the most important of all, and, as far as education is concerned, this means that it would be wise to invest more in the facilities and resources of primary schools where young children will reap the benefits. Technologically speaking, I would say a lot of our schools are behind the rest of the developed world. In Japan, for example, every classroom has at least one computer, as well as a projector screen and a number of other technology-driven interactive tools. It is vital, in this, the information age, that we introduce kids to technology as early as possible, and that's why I strongly feel that there is now a greater need than ever to kit out our primary schools with the latest gadgets. Besides, the children of the information age are becoming so accustomed to using technology in the other areas of their lives that they will more likely respond well to technology-based lessons than the traditional kind, which will ultimately see them learning more effectively, engaging more genuinely and developing more speedily.

ELEANOR B

People often groan about the faults of our education system, but I think we just like to complain; my gut feeling is that most people are actually only too aware of how lucky they are to have such a high quality of formal education open to them for free all the way up to the end of secondary school. What we take for granted — free education — is not something students from other parts of the world necessarily enjoy. The standard of teaching in our schools is also second-to-none. Another thing which can't be said everywhere. I mean, in Greece, for example, state school teachers are often so indifferent that students are forced to attend extra study classes at night — the cost of which has to be borne by their parents. Not alone is this a waste of money, it also eats into students' free time. The situation is similar in South Korea — students have private lessons in the evenings to help them improve their state school grades, and sometimes, between state school classes, private lessons and homework, there are literally not enough hours in the day, leading to exhaustion and burnout in a worst-case scenario, and, even in the best one, a significant reduction in the amount of leisure time available to pursue healthy activities and partake in the kind of fun and games that should characterize youth. In Britain, we go to school from 9 a.m. until 4 p.m.; we have the evening to enjoy being young and that is how it should be; to quote a well-known proverb, 'you're only young once'.

°ALAN D

I have a problem with the testing mechanisms used today. I mean, if you look at the statistics for the exams every year, there is one striking pattern; more and more people are getting As; the nation's results on average are getting better and better year-on-year. So, that means one of two things: either students today are smarter than ever before, or their examinations are watered down and do not represent a fair test. I personally believe the latter is true and I am incensed that this is being allowed to happen. In ten of fifteen years' time, it will have gotten to the stage where an A is meaningless if this continues. In order for the education system to be taken seriously, it is vital, therefore, that a complete overhaul of the examination system takes place and that we return to a situation where examinations offer a meaningful challenge and a true test of ability. That way, when a child receives an A, his or her achievement will feel genuine; it will have been earned and the child concerned will have the right to feel very proud of themselves. The problem is, in this country, we have forgotten that there is absolutely no shame in getting a B, or a C or D grade for that matter. Provided we do our best, that is always good enough. But, in this politically correct world-gone-mad of ours, assessors seem to think the only way forward is to give more and more of us the best grades, devaluing the grading system completely. It is as though they don't think we could take it if we got anything less than an A; as though we should all somehow be perfect students. The problem with that is that it is just not realistic, and, when you set unrealistic objectives, the only way to achieve them is to 'play' with the figures to manufacture the right results...

PART 1 Writing | **Question 1**

Read the two texts below.

Write an essay summarising and evaluating the key points from both texts. Use your own words throughout as far as possible, and include your own ideas in your answers.

Write your answer in **240-280** words.

1.

Mums owe it to their kids to stay at home.

Time and again, research has shown that the more attention children have from their parents, especially during the early years of life, the quicker and more assuredly they develop. Therefore, it seems to be a no-brainer that mothers should be encouraged, where at all possible, to stay at home. Indeed, unless there is a financial necessity for the mother to venture out into the workplace, to do so would otherwise be downright irresponsible and selfish. In cases where the father earns enough money to sustain his family on a single income, mothers should, therefore, be actively encouraged to tend to their children.

Kids from dual-income families grow up quicker.

According to the findings of a new study carried out in Denmark, children of families where both parents have jobs mature more quickly and exhibit more self-confidence at an earlier age than do those who come from backgrounds where one or both parents stay at home. This gives them a competitive edge over their pampered peers and increases the likelihood of their succeeding in later life, according to the report. Such children are also in general more proactive and driven, and are twice as likely to hold down a part-time job during after-school hours.

Write your **essay**.

PART 2 Writing | **Questions 2-4**

Write an answer to **one** of the questions **2-4** in this part. Write your answer in **280-320** words in an appropriate style on the separate answer sheet. Put the question number in the box at the top of the answer sheet.

2. A health magazine is running a series of reviews of restaurants which claim to provide healthy meal alternatives. You decide to send in a review in which you describe a recent visit to one such restaurant. Describe the range of foods on the menu, comment on the availability of so-called healthy options, mention the conclusions you drew from your own dining experience and say whether or not you would recommend this eatery to those looking for a healthy alternative.

Write your **review**.

3. You have just arrived back from a package holiday in the French Alps. Overall, you are very dissatisfied with your experience. You were particularly disappointed by the standard of accommodation, resort description and transport arrangements for getting to and from your hotel. You decide to write a letter to the travel agency with which you booked your holiday, outlining your grievances and stating what you expect the company to do about the situation.

Write your **letter**.

4. A magazine is running a series of articles on youth issues and this week's topic is youth crime. The magazine has invited readers to send in articles commenting on the situation in their local area. Contributors should outline the state of youth crime where they live, and provide their opinions about what they think the main causes are, how well authorities deal with the issue and put preventative measures in place, and what they believe should be done differently in order to alleviate the problem.

Write your **article**.

Listening

You will hear three different extracts. For questions 1-6, choose the answer (A, B, or C) which fits best according to what you hear. There are two questions for each extract.

EXTRACT 1

You hear a scientist giving a talk on research into the effects of global warming.

1. Why is the presence of Vibrios in the Baltic Sea significant in the context of this talk?
   A. it can lead to Vibrio infections
   B. the bacteria are usually found in tropical environments
   C. there is resultant warming of the water at a rate of 0.08 degrees per year

2. What can we conclude about the predicted influx of mosquitoes to the British Isles?
   A. it may lead to a rise in rates of illness in the general population
   B. it will not be dramatic as mosquitoes prefer warmer climates
   C. it will take a considerable length of time for it to happen

EXTRACT 2

You hear a reporter interviewing a scientist who has just completed an experiment.

3. What do we learn about the jellyfish the scientist created?
   A. it fulfilled all the criteria to be classed as a new life form
   B. it was created using only synthetic parts
   C. it relied on an animal heart for movement

4. What does the scientist say is the next step in his project?
   A. to find a means of giving the life form a degree of intelligence
   B. to train the experimental life form to seek energy and food
   C. to test the experimental life form's brain capacity and intelligence

EXTRACT 3

You hear a health consultant talking about health hazards presented by and in ladies' handbags.

5. What can we conclude from listening to the speaker?
   A. women should avoid carrying plastic bottles in their handbags
   B. drinking water on sale in plastic bottles poses a risk to health
   C. glass bottles are preferable to plastic bottles for regular re-use

6. What does the speaker say about make-up?
   A. it harbours bacteria similar to that found in food
   B. all mascara products are known to harm the area around the eye
   C. make-up products should be discarded after a year and a half

PART 2 Listening Questions 7-15

You will hear a journalist talking about the life of a famous country and western singer.
For questions 7-15 complete the sentences with a word or short phrase.

Wells' wholesome **7** [   ] did not, at first, seem a good fit with the

notion of her becoming a high profile supporter of women's rights.

Her first song was a **8** [   ] to Hank Thompson's lyric, *The Wild Side*

of Life, and struck a chord with female listeners.

Wells implied that married men were responsible for the extramarital affairs they had in an effort to

shield women who got involved in such relationships from **9** [   ].

Most of her hits were far less controversial and far more **10** [   ] than

It Wasn't God Who Made Honky Tonk Angels, and many touched on the subject of romance.

In **11** [   ] terms, Wells has not enjoyed the same success as a num-

ber of the female country and western singers who followed in her footsteps.

After her success began to wane, Wells looked into **12** [   ] in which

to take her career.

Wells foray into television made her **13** [   ] to a greater extent than

she had been before.

When she returned to producing music, she did so under the banner of a new

14 [   ].

The receipt of a Lifetime Achievement Award at the Grammys capped her career and represented her

15 [   ].

PART 3 Listening **Questions 16-20**

You will hear part of a discussion on a current affairs programme between Nick and Alison about the performance of the company Facebook since it floated on the stock exchange, hosted by Emily Dunne. For questions 16-20, choose the answer (A, B, C or D) which first best according to what you hear.

16 What does Alison think is cause for optimism?
   A. the company kept its costs low
   B. the loss generated was less than expected
   C. there appears to be good revenue potential
   D. the company hasn't started to advertise yet

17 According to Nick, the increasing popularity of smaller devices
   A. represents untapped potential for FACEBOOK.
   B. is a significant challenge to FACEBOOK increasing its revenue.
   C. puts FACEBOOK at a competitive advantage.
   D. gives the company an opportunity to advertise more.

18 In what situation does Alison believe FACEBOOK users might abandon the company?
   A. if they are given the option of watching adverts on certain apps and sites
   B. if a free social network becomes available on the net
   C. if the company pushes advertisements onto users too forcefully
   D. if sites and apps start to appear which put users off using FACEBOOK

19 What do we learn about the company's performance?
   A. the share price has now dropped by over one-third
   B. there has been a 6% improvement in the share price overnight
   C. $38 has been wiped off the share price
   D. it has become the biggest flop in history

20 Nick believes that Google
   A. will inevitably prevail over FACEBOOK in time.
   B. was short-sighted to invest everything it had into one project.
   C. technology will be made redundant by what FACEBOOK offers users.
   D. will become profit-making in a matter of time.

PART 4 Listening **Questions 21-30**

You will hear five short extracts in which London residents talk about how they came to be living there and how they feel about the city. You will hear the recording twice. While you listen, you must complete both tasks.

TASK ONE

For questions 21-25, choose from the list (A-H) what brought the speakers to London to begin with.

A a business trip
B a love interest
C it's their country of birth
D their family was seeking asylum
E an offer of employment in a hospital
F they were enrolled in a third-level institute
G economic reasons
H they were left an inheritance there

Speaker 1 [ ] 21
Speaker 2 [ ] 22
Speaker 3 [ ] 23
Speaker 4 [ ] 24
Speaker 5 [ ] 25

TASK TWO

For questions 26-30, choose from the list (A-H) how each speaker feels about living in London today.

A they consider London their true home
B they stay because their partner isn't keen on relocating
C they stay since it still makes financial sense
D they plan to stay at least ten years
E they have had enough of life there now
F they want to go back to London when they've grown up
G they find it quite a polluted city
H they may return to their home country after their children are reared

Speaker 1 [ ] 26
Speaker 2 [ ] 27
Speaker 3 [ ] 28
Speaker 4 [ ] 29
Speaker 5 [ ] 30

Test 7

Reading

PART 1 Reading | **Questions 1-8**

For questions 1-8, read the text below and decide which answer (A, B, C or D) best fits each gap. Mark your answers on the separate answer sheet. There is an example at the beginning (0).

Example   **0**   **A** thought   **B** expected   **C** predicted   **D** objected

| 0 | A | B | C | D |

Iconic Symbol Lost to Galapagos Forever

The news of the demise of Lonesome George, (0).......... to be the last-surviving member of his species, Geochelone abingdoni, is unlikely to come as a shock to those who (1)......... the fortunes of Galapagos, the habitat that inspired the Darwinian theory of evolution, and one that is now genuinely under real threat and in danger of being (2).......... harmed by human activity, with the main source of damage being tourism.

Early visitors to the archipelago were what could be (3).......... true nature-loving tourists, a group which did little collective or individual harm to the islands and did not interfere with the fragile balance of the ecosystem. However, in more recent times, eco-tourism has grown to enjoy almost cult-like popularity. Eco-tourists are a very different beast though and are rather more (4).......... in their tastes. Therefore, while, on the (5).......... of it, they come to marvel at the natural splendours the archipelago (6).......... , they do so only on the understanding that their comfort will not be sacrificed, requiring tour providers to take special measures to accommodate their more discerning tastes.

Large companies are best positioned to offer these eco-tourists the luxuries they have come to expect, but their popularity with visitors is sidelining local operators, a proportion of whose revenue goes towards the upkeep and conservation of the precious ecosystem. Sadly, the large international tour companies are far less benevolent with the (7).......... of their activities, which results in a double-edged sword situation whereby, due to larger numbers of tourists, more and more of the islands' habitat is being disturbed while, at the same time, less funding is being made available to conserve the ecosystem.

If the situation continues to (8)....... , Lonesome George may be but the first of many rare and endangered creatures to disappear.

1.	A track	B pursue	C observe	D grasp
2.	A irrespectively	B irreversibly	C irrelevantly	D irreverently
3.	A coined	B termed	C stated	D shared
4.	A delineating	B deliberating	C discriminating	D debilitating
5.	A front	B face	C cusp	D side
6.	A hosts	B lends	C boasts	D homes
7.	A results	B proceeds	C finances	D costs
8.	A deteriorate	B disrepair	C decompose	D distress

PART 3   Reading | **Questions 17-24**

For questions 17-24, read the text below. Use the word given in capitals at the end of the lines to form a word that fits in the space in the same line. There is an example at the beginning (0).
Write your answers **IN CAPITAL LETTERS** on the separate answer sheet.

Example: **0**   recourse

A Great Staycation

Holidays at home are usually a last **(0)** _recourse_; when all other options have been ruled out for one   COURSE

reason or another, but, in these tough times when money is perhaps tighter than ever before, the grim

(17)................................ that the stay-at-home vacation may be the only realistic **(18)**................................ is one   REAL/ ALTER

that more and more of us are faced with.

However, this does not have to mean a **(19)**................................ time in the same old **(20)**................................   MISERY/

you are in for the other 355-odd days of the year. For those willing to think outside the box a little, there   ROUND

are, in fact, a **(21)**................................ of possibilities that should be explored.   MULTIPLE

Ever thought about a house swap, for example? The house swap is the ultimate holiday **(22)**............................   RECEDE

buster. And there are now websites on which **(23)**................................ individuals, couples and families looking to   MIND

get a flavour of the life lived in someone else's home can hook up and start house swapping.

Okay, so it's not the two weeks in Gran Canaria you might have hoped for, but staying in someone else's

(24)................................ for a few days at least, whether it be ten, fifty or one hundred miles away, sure beats   RESIDE

slouching around at home on your own sofa.

PART 2   Reading | **Questions 9-16**

For questions 9-16 read the text below and think of the word which best fits each gap. Use only one word in each space. There is an example at the beginning (0).

Example: **0**   NOT

The New Invaders

(0)..._Not_... since the Spanish Conquest has an invasion on this **(9)**................................ so threatened Peru's precious Inca heritage. Today they come armed with backpacks and cameras rather than muskets and swords. Last year alone, of the country's 2.25 million foreign visitors, nearly half headed straight for Machu Picchu, **(10)**................................ thousands tromping along the ancient Inca Trail to get there.

In 2004, **(11)**................................ mounting pressure from Unesco, the Peruvian government took measures to protect the ancient site, setting a 500-a-day limit on the number of visitors allowed in. But this hasn't **(12)**................................ off tour companies out to make a quick buck, which openly flout the law and get around it by opening up new 'unofficial' hiking routes to the top.

Unesco has been infuriated by seeming government complicity in this behaviour. After all, the infamous Carrilluchayoc bridge, and others like it, which **(13)**................................ Machu Picchu up to hundreds of thousands of illegal visitors each year, could, quite easily, be blocked off by the state were it only to show an interest. Instead, it **(14)**................................ a blind eye as the situation escalates out of control.

And Unesco has finally **(15)**................................ its patience, demanding of the Peruvian government immediate action to stem the tide of unauthorised tourists whose careless, nitwitted trespass is putting the future of the ancient wonder **(16)**................................ threat.

PART 4 | Reading | Questions 25-30

For questions 25-30, complete the second sentence so that it has a similar meaning to the first sentence, using the word given. Do not change the word given. You must use between three and eight words, including the word given. Here is an example (0).

Example:

0   I think I just saw Frankie for a split second driving past in a Ferrari no less.   **caught**

I think I just .... for a split second driving past in a Ferrari no less.

Write only the missing words on the separate answer sheet.   **0 | caught sight of Frankie**

---

25. He refused to accept help and this led to his increasing isolation.

    down

    His increasing isolation .... to accept help.

26. His fake arrogance only hid his genuine insecurity.

    lay

    Behind .... insecurity.

27. Only the top fifteen players will make it through to the next round.

    advance

    The .... to the next round.

28. His side would have won the game had he not missed the penalty.

    prevented

    His missed .... the game.

29. The goalkeeper did not have to make a single save all game.

    without

    The game .... make a single save.

30. It is quite urgent that we hold this meeting.

    matter

    The meeting should .... urgency.

You are going to read an article about the female golfer Cheyenne Woods. For questions 31-36, choose the answer (A, B, C or D) which you think fits best according to the text. Mark your answers on the separate answer sheet.

Woods the Second

The resemblance is uncanny; the aura, unmistakable; as Cheyenne strides confidently up the fairway, there is no mistaking it; this is a Woods alright; the same eyes, elevated cheek bones and toothy grin; were it not for the long hair, you'd almost be forgiven for mistaking her profile for that of her legendary uncle, Tiger - in his prime. Tiger's father Earl is to thank not only for gifting his son to golf, then, but also, now it seems, instilling the same love of the game in his grandniece, who, when barely old enough to walk, he placed a club in the hand of and began to teach. It is as though history is repeating itself here; is another member of the Woods family about to take the world of golf by storm?

Well, if Cheyenne, now 21, has anything to do with it, don't be surprised. There may barely be enough room for one Tiger in the family, but this particular tigress won't stop until she has at least secured a small portion of the spotlight for herself. And, rest assured, the eyes of the golfing world are monitoring her progress with a keen sense of curiosity - mainly because the story, were it to unfold in the manner in which she hopes it will, is one that even Hollywood couldn't script.

It is almost inconceivable that another Woods could venture into the golfing world after Tiger – besides, is anyone else worthy or capable of carrying on the tradition of golfing supremacy synonymous with the Woods name? Tiger has monopolised the scoreboards of the U.S. Tour for so long; how does one follow that? And in the wake of his achievements, the pressure on Cheyenne must be immense, which might, perhaps, explain her poor debutant showing, when she missed the cut in her first tournament as a professional at the LPGA Championship earlier this year. Surely her every stroke is encumbered by the burden of responsibility that comes with trying to carry on the Woods' tradition.

At any rate, one somehow suspects Tiger is less than ready to pass on the baton just yet. Indeed, one wonders how he might feel about having another Woods out there competing in his arena. But perhaps, in light of his rather ignominious fall from grace in recent years following the release of the lurid details of his private life and the extent of his unfaithfulness to his ex-wife, he might well welcome the distraction Cheyenne creates. It may even make it easier for him to rebuild his game with the minimum of fuss and attention, away from the spotlight, as the wounded Tiger bides his time until he is ready to pounce again – and signs are that he will soon have the majors back within his sights, so that may not be very long at all now.

As for what Cheyenne thinks about all this newfound attention in her life, well, she is determined to be herself and is unlikely to be content to remain in Tiger's shadow; that much is sure. And while she may not emulate her illustrious uncle's trophy haul, nor come to dominate the sport as he did, she seems, at least, determined to give a good showing, and should her budding golfing career fall short of expectations, it will not have been for the want of trying because, from watching her on the practice ground during tournaments, it is clear that the famous Woods' work ethic has certainly rubbed off.

In truth, only the media will pitch these two against one another though - purely for dramatic value, as I am perhaps guilty of having done here. The reality is that Woods is none too bothered by what his young niece is up to, and, in fact, he likes to support her as and when he can, offering her advice on aspects of her game whenever the two cross paths, which, these days, with the busy tour schedule, is very seldom indeed. Similarly, Cheyenne is very keen not to be compared to her uncle, stating that 'not everyone can be Tiger Woods.' Indeed, her down-to-earth mentality and easy way with people are proof of this in one respect at least, for these attributes that went missing from the gene pool when her uncle was being brought into the world are qualities that she herself has in abundance.

Is Cheyenne likely to do for women's golf what Tiger did for men's during the 90s? Well, while not completely beyond the realms of possibility, you would have to say probably not. Are we likely to see the raucous crowds chant her name as she stalks the middle of the fairway on the final hole of a major championship for the umpteenth time, ready to pounce and claim another spectacular glory, constantly reaffirming her status alongside the near-superhuman elite of professional sport? Well, as she made no bones about declaring pretty forthrightly herself, not everyone can be Tiger Woods... But, then, Cheyenne isn't and harbours no desire to be her uncle anyway. She is her own person, and whatever type of career she forges in the end, it will have been forged in her own way, make no mistake about that. In truth, the early signs are that she will hardly set the world alight, but then, how can you dismiss a player with that unmistakably Woods-esque glint in the eye. She will probably hate me for saying this, but Cheyenne Woods very definitely has the eye of the Tiger, and, with that in her arsenal, anything could happen...

31. **Based on the information provided in the opening paragraph, it is clear**

     A. that Cheyenne Woods has developed features strikingly similar to the way her uncle looks today.

     B. that both Cheyenne Woods and her uncle have the same family member to thank for introducing them to the game of golf.

     C. that three generations of the Woods family shared very similar physical features in their youth.

     D. that both Cheyenne and Tiger Woods feel deeply grateful to Tiger's father Earl for his role in introducing them to the game of golf.

32. **Of the pressure Cheyenne Woods is under,**

     A. the writer suggests this may have been a factor which contributed to the poor manner in which she kicked off her professional career.

     B. the writer feels that it is lessened by the sheer scale of the achievements of Tiger, as no one could realistically expect her to emulate him.

     C. the writer suggests that she coped admirably with it at the LPGA Championship earlier in the year, considering the fact that she was just a debutant.

     D. the writer suggests that she has openly admitted that she is severely encumbered by the burden of trying to follow in her uncle's footsteps.

33. **What does the writer NOT imply about Cheyenne's uncle, Tiger Woods?**

     A. He may be relieved that Cheyenne is taking some of the attention away from him.

     B. He is close to returning to his best form on the golf course.

     C. He fell out of favour with members of the public after details of his private life were revealed.

     D. He has never courted attention and throughout his years of success has been keen to stay out of the spotlight.

34. **What do we learn about Cheyenne's approach to golf?**

     A. She expects to be able to emulate the achievements of her uncle.

     B. She wants to be a very dominant figure in her sport.

     C. Her work ethic is something she has in common with her uncle Tiger.

     D. She wants to try to bring her good form on the practice ground into her tournament play more often.

35. **What is said about a potential rivalry between the two Woods players, Tiger and Cheyenne?**

     A. This is a figment of the imagination of journalists.

     B. The pair are keen for this rivalry to intensify.

     C. The pair are too busy competing in tournaments to allow it to distract them.

     D. While Tiger is supportive of Cheyenne, she is less keen to endorse her uncle.

36. **What is implied in the final paragraph?**

     A. So far, the evidence points to a strong likelihood that Cheyenne will be an extremely successful golfer.

     B. Although it seems unlikely that Cheyenne will emulate her uncle, it would be a mistake to completely discount someone with such a good pedigree.

     C. Cheyenne is an unpredictable and volatile player and anything could happen as far as her future in the game of golf is concerned.

     D. Cheyenne has high expectations of herself and is pretty forthright about declaring her intentions.

PART 6   Reading | **Questions 37-43**

You are going to read a magazine article. Seven paragraphs have been removed from the article. Choose from the paragraphs A-H the one which fits each gap (37-43). There is one extra paragraph you do not need to use. Mark your answers on the separate answer sheet.

The Importance of Being Dad

New dad, Rowan Daniel Foote, is in far from familiar territory here, and discovers, while researching this piece, that being a father is anything but straight-forward.

What separates the good dad from the bad? By what parameters do we define 'good dad' anyway? What is the baseline? Is it a case of good dad changes the nappies while bad dad watches T.V.? If only it were this simple.

37

Only recently, an Oxford research team linked the absence of an early-years father figure with a predisposition in adolescent girls towards the development of mental health problems, likely to significantly limit the affected teens' ability to meet their full potential later in life. Similarly, boys who do not have a credible father figure in their lives are more likely to get on the wrong side of the law, and, for both sexes, the presence of a 'good dad' provides for greater motivation to perform academically, so kids are likely to excel more at school when dad is an active rather than passive participant.

38

Whether it is biological dad or stepdad is, according to the findings of the Oxford team, neither here nor there, suggesting that a biological attachment and innate sense of affinity and desire to bond is the exclusive domain of the mother. The key to a child's level of happiness is the extent of its involvement with whichever manifestation of dad circumstances conspire to present.

39

So, we have established that dad needs to be hands on in his approach, but from day one, in year one, during the terrible twos, from three and up, in the early years, during the teenage years ... basically when exactly?

40

Now, that is not to say that 'the ouchies' (ages 1-4 – think first steps, little spills, big spills ... lots of tears), 'the naughties' (ages 5-12, when the mischief-making starts in earnest...) and the 'do-the-exact-opposite-of-whatever-mummy-and-daddy-tell-me-ies' (the, ehem, teenage years...) aren't important times for which daddy should be around too, but the findings do suggest that an extra effort should be made to be present and involved as much as possible in those first few months of life.

41

For dad it can be hard too – and frustrating to see how easily the bond between mother and baby is formed. But there are things he can do to try to forge a meaningful bond of his own. Simple acts like nappy-changing and bathing can make all the difference, and even a possessive mother will soon tire of having to do these chores by herself, and will eventually welcome the extra pair of hands with her arms wide open. Even feeding does not have to be monopolised by mum, who can facilitate here by expressing her milk to afford dad the opportunity to get involved, too. Besides, many babies, whether for reasons of personal preference of the parents or out of necessity, are bottle fed, which presents far fewer complications for the willing would-be feeder-dad.

42

Mind-altering fluffy chemicals aside though, there's no doubt that dads have it tough today. Theirs is a constantly changing role, and many new fathers undergo an identity crisis of sorts just trying to define for themselves exactly what their purpose should be. Gone are the days of dad simply being the breadwinner, but stay-at-home dads are equally rare. Most fathers have to juggle a full-time job with their strong desire to contribute at home, often fighting off tiredness and frustration, and pushing their bodies to the limit just to be there for their children.

43

This can be a source of frustration for mums, too, who are often left feeling isolated and literally 'holding the baby'. They often crave adult company and will naturally turn to dad to take over when he arrives home in the evening, whether dad is of a mind to help out or not after his long day. Communication is therefore an essential part of the equation for new parents; they must speak with one another and develop a plan which affords both of them at least some break time to recharge their batteries and keep them functioning well. Failure to do this will result not only in their own health suffering, but, potentially, that of their baby also.

A

That last point is interesting because it also has implications for children from broken homes; basically, what the research suggests is that whether dad is 'real dad', 'new dad' or 'visit-three-times-a-week-as-part-of-the-divorce-conditions-dad' is of little relevance; so long as 'whatever dad' is properly involved in his child's upbringing and is a stable and constant influence, 'any dad' will do just fine, once he is prepared to carry out his role and take on the responsibility of parenthood. On the other hand, 'shirker dads' of any ilk, be they biological, step, occasional or who knows, as a direct result of their lack of engagement with the parenting role, cause permanent damage to the children in their care.

B

Apart from making a concerted effort to get involved, dad should also try to understand that bonds take time to form, and, oftentimes, it is only a matter of persevering - though, thankfully, most men do not have to wait too long before their feigned or conscious effort to show interest in the baby becomes far more genuine and instinctive. Increased levels of the prolactin hormone will usually see to this. As another study revealed, levels of the so-called 'cuddle chemical' usually increase dramatically in new dads, which is nature's way of rewiring pop's brain for its new role in fatherhood.

C

Well, just as is the case with mother and child, the Oxford study found that it is during the first year of life – 'the noughties' (the 12 months it takes to get from zero to one) – that it is most important to develop the bond between father and baby. The offspring of a father actively involved in personal care in that period is less likely to develop behavioural problems as a teen, and has the best chance of going on to become a well-rounded individual in later life.

D

Ultimately, what you give your child will be returned with interest in later years; you get out of parenting what you put in. If you want your child to grow up into a well-balanced and successful adult, then it is vital to afford them as much of your attention as possible, especially in the teenage years, which are undoubtedly the most important of all when it comes to the extent and effects of a father's influence.

E

Their plight is not much helped by our archaic and heartless employment laws either, which afford male workers little paid leave to spend time with their new-born kids, forcing them to work long hours during the day only to have to come home to do another shift looking after the baby, and to perhaps then have to endure a less-than-perfect night's sleep into the bargain.

F

We place huge importance on the role of motherhood during the formative years of a child's life, heaping bucket loads of unnecessary pressure on an already dazed mum who is wondering just what she has let herself in for, and who doesn't need grandma and aunties Maureen and Peg adding their tuppence worth of advice into the bargain. But, in doing so, we very often overlook the father's role. This despite the fact that research has consistently shown us that daddy's influence, or lack thereof, has just as pivotal a role to play in the development, for better or for worse, of his child.

G

The study even found a link between the prospect of marital success and the degree of involvement of the father of the newlywed during childhood; the more heightened this degree, it seems, the more likely one's marriage will succeed. In short, dad is critical from day one, and he has to be prepared to make time to spend time with his children no matter how much sacrifice that entails.

H

But, truth told, that is easier said than done. After all, mummy has been carrying her little package around with her for nine months by the time it pops out onto the delivery table, so she has had nearly a year's head start in having the sensation – and constant reminder – of parenthood. Besides, given the strength of the maternal instinct in most women, an unwillingness to share the experience, even with the person with whom the package was so intimately created, is not atypical. It is up to mum, then, to guard against being overprotective and to encourage her partner to play a meaningful role from as early as possible, preferably from the very first moment little bundle is brought into its new home.

You are going to read the transcript of a series of interviews with ordinary people conducted for the *Have your say* feature of a daily newspaper. For questions 44-53, choose from the people (**A-D**). The people may be chosen more than once.

Mark your answers on the separate answer sheet.

Which person gives each of these opinions about the economic crisis?

A culture of trying to look for people to blame for our problems is what caused the crisis in the first place.   **44** ☐

People feel helpless to change the situation and this is reflected in their lack of interest in the political system.   **45** ☐

It was glaringly obvious that the bottom would fall out of the housing market, not just to experts but to everyone.   **46** ☐

Some form of civil disturbance or protest by ordinary members of the public is likely if the economic crisis continues.   **47** ☐

It is very unfair that the people in finance who caused our economic problems continue to be well rewarded for their work while ordinary hard-working people suffer.   **48** ☐

Political parties should not receive funds from private sources but should instead be entirely state-funded.   **49** ☐

The highest earners should be required to pay more tax in order to generate more revenue for the government.   **50** ☐

The fact that some politicians tried to defraud the state by claiming more expenses than they were due is evidence that corruption is widespread in our society.   **51** ☐

There is very little difference in terms of policies between all of the main political parties today.   **52** ☐

We should stop trying to vilify bankers and take a more positive and proactive approach to speed up the economic recovery.   **53** ☐

CPE Practice Test 7

Have your say ... on the Economic Crisis

Robert

I find it infuriating to reflect on the fact that bankers, at least the ones at the top, continue to be paid huge sums of money every year and receive massive bonuses despite the fact that they are largely responsible for the poor state of health of the economy, and, let's not forget, the toughest and longest recession since the 1930s. I mean, where is the justice in that? While ordinary decent folk are losing their jobs and struggling to put food on the table as a result of problems that are no fault of their own, the very problem-makers themselves continue to earn big bucks. I wouldn't be surprised if there was an increase in civil unrest in the coming months and years, especially if the economic crisis continues to hit ordinary people hard. After all, if no one is going to look after their interests, they will have to start looking after their own — don't be surprised to see protest marches in the near future, and where there are large groups of unhappy people gathered together, there is always a danger that the situation will descend into chaos. I would never condone violence, but I think that the more desperate people get, the more I can empathise with why they might resort to it. If you are a man who has been unemployed for over a year, and who has to look on helplessly as his family disintegrates right before his very eyes, it must be awful — these people need help.

Barbara

The solution to our problems is very simple and I blame the political system for it not having happened already. Politicians, you see, are totally reliant on rich business people to bankroll their efforts to get elected. Now, ask yourself this, why on earth would a businessperson donate money to a politician out of the goodness of their heart? I mean, are we really so naive as to believe that that can actually happen. Well, just in case, let me put you straight — it can't and it doesn't. The only reason businesspeople give money to politicians is in return for favours when they get into power. And that's the problem. We now have a situation where the government doesn't have enough money to cover spending. The logical thing to do then would be to increase taxes to generate more, and obviously this obligation to pay extra tax should fall on those who earn the most — ah, but this is where we get into problem territory. You can't really expect politicians to vote to increase the tax rate of those who support them financially. To do so would be to risk angering their backers and losing their support, putting the very careers of the politicians themselves in jeopardy. Politicians clearly have a vested interest in maintaining low tax rates for the wealthy. The only way we are ever going to create a situation where this is not so is if we ban all private donations to political parties and fund them instead with money from the state's coffers. In the long run, it will work out less expensive — just think of all the money that would be saved as a result of there being less corruption — we might finally have politicians who focused on doing what's best for the country rather than on trying to prolong their political careers by doing favours for their 'buddies'.

Ned

It is not just the economy that is in crisis; it is the whole of society. The extent to which we have lost hope is, I think, reflected in voter apathy. Every time there is an election now, the number of people who turn out to vote is less and less. Surely this is a sign that people feel totally disenfranchised — powerless to make a difference. But, more importantly, it is an indictment of our politicians and the extent to which they have failed us. The people no longer see a point in voting as it won't make any real difference either way. Besides, nowadays, all the main parties have centrist policies; the whole political system might just as well join together into one big party and then we wouldn't even have to hold elections anymore. People often complain about the bankers and how they acted corruptly, and that this was the main cause of the economic crisis we are in today. Okay, fine; the bankers were definitely at fault, but they hardly have a monopoly on corruption. I mean, think about the expenses scandal from a couple of years ago — politicians were trying to claim huge sums of money they weren't entitled to; let's not kid ourselves; the whole system from the top down is corrupt, not just the bankers. They are just being made a scapegoat.

Mary

I think, today, that we live in a very cynical world. Everyone is very quick to point the finger of blame for our economic woes on anyone but themselves — the easy targets usually; the politicians, the bankers and so on. It is so easy to criticise other people and wash your hands of responsibility for what is happening. But that is what got us into this mess in the first place — people not taking responsibility for their actions. The way I see it, it is about time that we all started to take a little bit of responsibility and instead of blaming the rest of the world for our problems, perhaps we should start by looking at ourselves. Okay, so the bankers did wrong; they were careless with money, but so were we. Who put a gun to your head and made you buy a house that was so overpriced it was obvious there was going to be a dramatic downward correction? Is it the bank's fault or your own that you are in negative equity now? Now, just because you made a mistake with your money doesn't mean you are some kind of monster — and the same goes for the bankers... Let's stop trying to find scapegoats and instead try to work together to pull ourselves out of this crisis. We do not need the cynicism of naysayers, we need people to think positively and try to make good things happen to get this recovery underway. I for one am done with the blame game.

Writing

PART 1   Writing   **Question 1**

Read the two texts below.

Write an essay summarising and evaluating the key points from both texts. Use your own words throughout as far as possible, and include your own ideas in your answers.

Write your answer in **240-280** words.

1.

Longevity poses series Headaches

It is becoming the greatest social issue of our time – how exactly should society deal with the fact that people are living longer? The extended life expectancy of the elderly is causing headaches for the government and individuals alike, by putting a strain on the healthcare and welfare systems, not to mention testing the financial limits of grown-up children, keen to do well by their elderly parents but struggling to pay the astronomical rates charged by private care homes, and who also face the difficulty of trying to find time to spend with their mothers and fathers while holding down a full-time job and raising kids of their own.

The Changing Dynamics of the Home

There was a time when it was commonplace for grandparents to live with and be looked after by the rest of the family, but, today, this is the exception rather than the rule. Parents struggle to cope with bringing up their own children, never mind caring for their folks into the bargain. They have little choice but to put them in a home where they can get the care and attention that they need and deserve. Besides, such is the generational divide between children and their grandparents today that the idea of the two living under the one roof is simply not going to work anymore.

Write your **essay**.

PART 2 Writing | **Questions 2-4**

Write an answer to **one** of the questions **2-4** in this part. Write your answer in **280-320** words in an appropriate style on the separate answer sheet. Put the question number in the box at the top of the answer sheet.

2. A health magazine is running a series of reviews of restaurants which claim to provide healthy meal alternatives. You decide to send in a review in which you describe a recent visit to one such restaurant. Describe the range of foods on the menu, comment on the availability of so-called healthy options, mention the conclusions you drew from your own dining experience and say whether or not you would recommend this eatery to those looking for a healthy alternative.

    Write your **review**.

3. Your friend has asked you for a character reference, which has been requested by a prospective employer. She is hoping to secure a part-time morning job working with children in a creche. Write a letter to the attention of the creche owner stating for how long the two of you have been friends, outlining the positive attributes your friend possesses and explaining, in your view, why she would be a suitable candidate for the role.

    Write your **letter**.

4. Your manager feels that customer service levels at your company have been slipping for some time and has asked you to write a report on the issue, for which you were first required to conduct a customer feedback survey. Using the results you have collected from the feedback survey, write the report, outlining the main issues customers have highlighted, the underlying causes of these problems, and what can be done to improve the level of service customers receive going forward.

    Write your **report**.

Listening

You will hear three different extracts. For questions 1-6, choose the answer (A, B, or C) which fits best according to what you hear. There are two questions for each extract.

EXTRACT 1

You hear a lecturer in the science department of a university talking to students about critical thinking.

1. What is the speaker trying to emphasise?
   A. the relevance of normative perspectives
   B. the importance of following scientific convention
   C. the need to be imaginative in the way we think

2. What is the speaker's point about the conventional policy for dealing with siblings up for adoption?
   A. it is well-intentioned but critically flawed
   B. it puts people off the adoption process altogether
   C. it is too complex and confuses prospective adopters

EXTRACT 2

You hear part of a radio interview with a behavioural scientist related to the role fathers play in the development of young children.

3. What can be implied about the father's role in the development of young children?
   A. the extent of his involvement is of little significance
   B. young girls benefit most from greater interaction with their fathers
   C. boys are more adversely affected by the absence of a father figure

4. What evidence did researchers find to suggest young children with involved fathers develop better?
   A. such children interact more with the world around them
   B. such children tend to vocalise their needs by crying a lot
   C. such children tend to sleep for longer periods at a time

EXTRACT 3

You hear an education consultant talking about the introduction of a new type of school system at secondary level.

5. What do we learn about the new 'studio schools'?
   A. they are run by powerful businesses
   B. they will offer an unconventional style of learning
   C. many are opening up permanently in towns across the U.K.

6. What do we learn about the general curriculum of 'studio schools'?
   A. optional work experience is available
   B. traditional academic subjects are not offered
   C. courses are high in practical content

PART 2 Listening   Questions 7-15

You will hear a golf reporter talking about the special association a well-known player had with a certain golf course. For questions 7-15 complete the sentences with a word or short phrase.

The golfer Severiano Ballesteros enjoyed [**7** _____] with Lytham and St Annes golf course throughout his career.

Ballesteros was confident of winning the [**8** _____] at Lytham on account of his excellent sand play.

That Ballesteros recovered in two shots from a bunker on fourteen of the fifteen occasions he found himself in one is [**9** _____] to his powers of recovery.

Spectators may have thought they had cause to be concerned by his wayward [**10** _____] on the sixteenth hole.

In order to get a good [**11** _____] towards the green, Ballesteros had deliberately aimed to slice his drive.

He went around the course in a very [**12** _____] manner and seldom landed in the middle of the fairway.

Ballesteros was never able to rid himself of [**13** _____] he got as a result of his wild play at Lytham.

Ballesteros' [**14** _____] had no leg left to stand on after his second win at Lytham proved his versatility and brilliance as a player.

His scintillating play went some way towards repaying the belief his legions [**15** _____] had shown in him.

PART 3 Listening   Questions 16-20

You will hear part of a discussion between two experts in linguistics, Jay Ore and Toll Keane, about learning foreign languages, facilitated by Miriam Potsbarn. For questions 16-20, choose the answer (A, B, C or D) which first best according to what you hear.

16   What do we learn about the speakers' foreign language credentials?
   A. Both men are fluent in all the foreign languages they've studied.
   B. The woman is presently studying Spanish.
   C. Both men are fluent in at least three languages.
   D. Two of the speakers claim not to be proficient in a language they learned.

17   What do the two men suggest about language learning?
   A. Success is largely dependent on the quality of teaching.
   B. There is no substitute for effort.
   C. The process of learning a language is a life-long one.
   D. A desire to speak many languages is more than enough.

18   In what sense is quality of teaching important?
   A. Teachers can act as facilitators to speed up learning.
   B. Good teachers motivate their students.
   C. Bad teachers create sceptical students.
   D. Bad teachers can turn motivated students off learning.

19   The two male speakers have designed a course that
   A. focuses on grammar and structure initially.
   B. initially immerses students in a second-language environment.
   C. enables students to make progress and see results quickly.
   D. is seldom taught in the language being learned.

20   What happens after the first three weeks of the course?
   A. Learners are no longer shown how they are progressing.
   B. There is a shift to a more conventional style of learning.
   C. The focus of teaching switches to basic practical language.
   D. Learners recognise their closeness to attaining fluency.

PART 4 Listening   Questions 21-30

You will hear five short extracts in which new film releases are reviewed. You will hear the recording twice. While you listen, you must complete both tasks.

TASK ONE
For questions 21-25, choose from the list (A-H) what is said about the director of each movie.

A their plot changes are not welcome	**Speaker 1**	21
B they had a very small budget to work with		
C they have dealt with difficult cast members well	**Speaker 2**	22
D they struggled to get on with their cast	**Speaker 3**	23
E they have created a thought-provoking film		
F they have documented real-life events	**Speaker 4**	24
G they have also written a related novel		
H their movie has been translated into Norwegian	**Speaker 5**	25

TASK TWO
For questions 26-30, choose from the list (A-H) what the reviewer's conclusion is.

A this is a good, uplifting movie	**Speaker 1**	26
B this movie does the original proud		
C this movie should have had a higher age rating	**Speaker 2**	27
D too much money was spent on the film	**Speaker 3**	28
E read the book before you see this movie		
F this movie will not look as good on T.V.	**Speaker 4**	29
G minors will probably not be allowed to watch this movie		
H this movie does not remain true to the original story	**Speaker 5**	30

Test 8

Reading

PART 1   Reading | **Questions 1-8**

For questions 1-8, read the text below and decide which answer (A, B, C or D) best fits each gap. Mark your answers on the separate answer sheet. There is an example at the beginning (0).

Example   **0 A.** indication   **B.** mechanism   **C.** obligation   **D.** invention

A LANGUAGE EXPERIMENT

Language is thought to be a(n) (0)........ for transmitting the information within thoughts. One experiment used to demonstrate this idea (1).......... subjects to listen to a short passage of several sentences, then to repeat the passage. Most people will accurately convey the (2).......... of the passage in the sentences they produce, but will not come close to repeating the sentences verbatim. It appears that two (3).......... are occurring. Upon hearing the passage, the subjects convert the language of the passage into a more abstract representation of its meaning, which is more easily (4).......... within memory. Then in order to recreate the passage, the subject (5).......... this representation and converts its meaning back into language.

This separation of thought and language is less intuitive than it might be because language can be a powerful (6).......... with which to manipulate thoughts. It provides a mechanism to internally rehearse, critique and (7).......... thoughts. This internal form of communication is (8).......... for a social animal and could certainly be, in part, responsible for the strong selective pressures for improved language use.

1.	A. requires	B. obtains	C. demands	D. promotes
2.	A. hunch	B. hub	C. gist	D. precision
3.	A. transformations	B. instigations	C. iterations	D. applications
4.	A. stored	B. reminded	C. acquired	D. retrieved
5.	A. supplies	B. discovers	C. reveals	D. recalls
6.	A. boon	B. prompt	C. tool	D. motive
7.	A. obscure	B. modify	C. reflect	D. accept
8.	A. incidental	B. insignificant	C. essential	D. definitive

PART 2   Reading   **Questions 9-16**

For questions 9-16 read the text below and think of the word which best fits each gap. Use only one word in each space. There is an example at the beginning (0).

Example: **0**   for

IN SUPPORT OF LANGUAGE DIVERSITY

There are solid reasons **(0)** ...**for**...... supporting, preserving, and documenting endangered languages. First, each and **(9)** .... language is a celebration of the rich cultural diversity of our planet; second, each language is an expression of a unique ethnic, social, regional or cultural identity and world view; third, language is the repository **(10)** .... the history and beliefs of a people; and finally, every language encodes a particular subset of fragile human knowledge **(11)** .... agriculture, botany, medicine and ecology.

(12) .... a doubt, mother tongues are comprised of far more **(13)** .... grammar and words. For example, Thangmi, a Tibeto-Burman language spoken by an ethnic community of around 30,000 people in eastern Nepal, is a mine of unique indigenous terms for local flora and fauna that have medical and ritual value. Much of this local knowledge is falling **(14)** .... disuse as fluency in Nepali, the national language, increases. **(15)** .... children cease to speak their mother tongue, the oral transmission of specific ethnobotanical and medical knowledge also **(16)** .... to an end.

PART 3   Reading   **Questions 17-24**

For questions 17-24, read the text below. Use the word given in capitals at the end of the lines to form a word that fits in the space in the same line. There is an example at the beginning (0).
Write your answers **IN CAPITAL LETTERS** on the separate answer sheet.

Example: **0**   conspiracy

JULIET: FAKN DEATH. C U LATR. ROMEO: GUD PLAN

Fancy some sort of **(0)**..**conspiracy**.... with a distant boyfriend or girlfriend? Send a text. Lost in the woods, **(17)**............................. , or a heavy fog? Use GPS. A case of mistaken identity? Facebook! And who is this **(18)**.................................. Jay Gatsby? Just Google him.	CONSPIRE WILD ENIGMA
Books can now be read on iPhones, and **(19)**...................................... young writers in Japan are using their cellphone keypads to write best-selling short novels. But, at the same time, technology is making some classic narrative plot devices obsolete. Excuses like poor connections and **(20)**......................................, or the **(21)**................................. to reach someone just don't work when even the most **(22)**....................................... places have wireless **(23)**.................................. .	OPPORTUNITY COMMUNICATE ABLE ACCESS / COVER
It's the same problem with movies. In *Casablanca*, Humphrey Bogart would have been spared the aching **(24)**..................................... of wondering why Ingrid Bergman stood him up at the train station. "Why isn't she here? We were supposed to run away together! Let me check my messages. Maybe I can find her online..."	CERTAIN

PART 4   Reading   **Questions 25-30**

For questions 25-30, complete the second sentence so that it has a similar meaning to the first sentence, using the word given. Do not change the word given. You must use between three and eight words, including the word given. Here is an example (0).

Example:

0   I think I just saw Frankie for a split second driving past in a Ferrari no less.   caught

     I think I just .... for a split second driving past in a Ferrari no less.

Write only the missing words on the separate answer sheet. | 0 | caught sight of Frankie |

---

25. There were plenty of people there to help us so the job got done quickly.

    lack

    The job got done quickly because .... help .

26. Your gift is so generous that I do not feel like I can accept it.

    possibly

    I .... generous gift.

27. Everything about the film was good but we were mostly impressed by the photography.

    impressive

    The photography .... the film.

28. Mandy has never forgotten to bring a snack.

    remember

    Mandy .... a snack.

29. Everyone in the company is hard-working, including Bob.

    anyone

    Bob is .... in the company.

30. The time that must be invested in development is the only drawback of this software.

    aside

    This software .... its lengthy development time.

PART 4   Reading   **Questions 25-30**

*You are going to read an extract about cyclist Lance Armstrong. For questions **31 - 36**, choose the answer (**A, B, C** or **D**) which you think fits best according to the text.*

Livestrong — but will the legacy?

In the early- to mid-1990s, Lance Armstrong was on the up-and-up. Success seemed to be written in his stars; he notched up a stage win at the '93 Tour de France, then another in '95. This cyclist was clearly coming of age in the sport, and he was, at 24 on registering his second tour win, still a relative baby in cycling terms - most of his career lay ahead of him. Then, just when it looked like he would conquer all before him, his '96 tour was cut disappointingly short due to illness. And, as it would soon emerge, this was no ordinary illness; Armstrong had testicular cancer. Fans were aghast and there was an outpouring of sympathy for him.

But Armstrong would need more than goodwill to get through this. The cancer had metastasized to the lungs and the brain. The prognosis was not at all good. Months of spirit- and body-breaking chemotherapy followed and a delicate surgical procedure to remove the malignancies on his brain was performed. Cycling mourned the surely permanent loss to the sport of one of its most promising young disciples. But Armstrong had other ideas.

In 1998, he made a remarkable, defiant and inspirational return to cycling and competed in the Tour de France again the following year. But surely his would now only be a cameo role; after all, what could one expect from a cancer survivor with a compromised liver and the other familiar scars of cancer therapy? Except Armstrong had other ideas. Four stage wins later, the legend of Armstrong was born; he had claimed the Tour and defied the odds in the most emphatic of manners. His victory represented not just his announcement as a force in cycling, but as a force for hope for millions of cancer sufferers the world over. Indeed, Armstrong threw himself into campaigning for his newly-established cancer foundation, Livestrong - so much so that he metamorphosed into a sort of human-embodiment of the cause – he became the cause, and his annual battle with the French Alps came to represent the struggle against the deadly disease. So long as Lance could succeed, there was hope.

And succeed he did, beyond the wildest expectations of even the most optimistic of his supporters, amassing a further six titles – so seven in consecution – before he retired in 2005. His achievements were simply remarkable; his story absorbing; his book a must-read for all cancer sufferers – their ray of hope; proof that hopefulness should never fade and that sanguinity can and does make light of the odds - the tunnel, though long and at times excruciating to pass through, has an end, and it is a happy one – the light is in sight.

After his seventh victory, he retired and the sporting world entered congratulatory mode, writing his eulogies. But Armstrong had one more surprise for us; he wasn't finished yet. There were whispers of a comeback, confirmed in 2009, and so it was that the legend would ride again.

But the renewed focus on him wasn't all good; there were whispers of another kind, too; sources, some credible, were claiming he had had an illicit ally all through his exploits; he was, they claimed, in bed with the syringe. Our champion laughed off and dismissed these claims but the rumours persisted and a cloud began to form over his legacy. Surely Armstrong could not have earned his victories clean, some said.

We may never know for sure. Fast-forward to 2012 and despite an abandoned federal case, those sharpening their knives for Armstrong seem to have finally nabbed him; ASADA, the U.S. body tasked with cracking down on drug offenders charged Armstrong with the doping and trafficking of drugs - and some say his failure to contest is indicative of his guilt. At any rate, because he pleaded no-contest, he will now be stripped of all his titles; his legacy has been pulled from under him.

And yet he has not, and now may never be tried, so we have not seen the evidence against him. We do not know if he is guilty or innocent, and it still remains fact that he never failed an official drugs test. Did he cheat? Does it matter? Does anyone care? Time may tell, but for now, though his legacy is tainted, his legend, in the eyes of many of his loyal supporters, lives on.

31. What does the writer mean when he says in the first paragraph that Lance Armstrong was 'coming of age in the sport'?

    A. he was of the right age to be a competitive cyclist

    B. he was nearly at the age at which it is expected that a cyclist should win

    C. he was of a mature age for a cyclist and had few years left in the sport

    D. he was beginning to figure as a real contender in his sport

32. Which of the following statements is true about the cancer Armstrong had?

    A. he recovered remarkably quickly from it, suffering little

    B. it started in the lungs and spread to the brain

    C. doctors were optimistic about his chances of survival

    D. the generally held view was that it would prevent him from cycling professionally ever again

33. Why does the writer say, 'Except Armstrong had other ideas', at the end of the third paragraph?

    A. Armstrong was determined to play some role in the Tour de France again

    B. Armstrong's idea of victory had changed since he'd had cancer.

    C. Armstrong was determined to defy the odds and become a real contender in the Tour de France.

    D. Armstrong didn't want to race for victory, he just wanted to represent cancer victims.

34. What does the writer compare Armstrong's Tour de France campaign struggle each year after his return to the sport with?

    A. the general fight against cancer

    B. a cancer organisation

    C. his fundraising for cancer

    D. Armstrong's own personal cancer experience

35. What is one of the ways in which his story became about more than just cycling?

    A. his published biography became a source of inspiration for cancer sufferers

    B. cycling through a tunnel was like fighting cancer

    C. he gave people hope that they could one day be professional athletes, too

    D. he gave people the belief to fight the disease that is drug-taking in sport

36. What can be inferred about the rumours of Armstrong's drug-taking?

    A. they were disproved in a state court case

    B. they have not caused Armstrong's reputation and record any harm

    C. they were eventually proved true beyond doubt

    D. he had, but passed up, an opportunity to disprove them

You are going to read an article about a system of writing used by the blind and the man who invented it. Seven paragraphs have been removed from the article. Choose from the paragraphs A - H the one which fits each gap (37 - 43). There is one extra paragraph which you do not need to use.

Louis Braille and the Braille System

Louis Braille's early life was ordinary. He was born on January 4, 1809, in the village of Coupvray, which lies approximately 50 kilometers east of Paris, France. His father, Simon-Rene Braille, was a saddler; his mother, Monique Baron, was the daughter of an agricultural labourer. Louis had three older siblings, two sisters and a brother. Louis, the fourth child, arrived 11 years after the birth of the third child.

37

What happened next was particularly unlucky for young Louis. Although the village had a doctor and a chemist, he did not receive effective treatment. The exact course of Louis' treatment is not known, but it is known that the injured eye became infected and was not surgically removed immediately. The infection spread, via the optic nerve, to the other eye and Louis lost sight in both eyes.

38

The Institute taught blind students a method of reading known as embossing. Large letters with raised outlines were printed so the outlines could be traced with fingers. But the size of the letters made the embossed books so large and expensive that only a few were available.

39

However, it was not Louis Braille who invented the first form of writing by means of dots. This invention is attributed to Charles Barbier, who was an artillery officer. He developed an interest in rapid, secret writing, as it pertains to matters of war, where speed and secrecy are mandatory.

40

Louis was about 12 years old when Charles Barbier brought his writing system to the school. Louis

immediately saw the potential, as well as the problems with the system. Over the next three years, Louis worked on simplifying the system, which is how the 6-dot braille system came into being. After that was accomplished, Louis eventually evolved his new system to include notation for numbers and music.

41

Its popularity may be attributed to the ease with which it can be used. Raised dots represent the letters of the alphabet, as well as equivalents for punctuation marks and letter groupings. Braille is read by moving the hand or hands from left to right along each line. Both hands are usually involved in the reading process, and reading is generally done with the index fingers. The average reading speed is about 125 words per minute, but greater speeds of up to 200 words per minute are possible.

42

By using Braille, blind people can benefit from increased educational opportunities. It provides a tool with which they can review and study the written word. They can become aware of different writing conventions such as spelling, punctuation, paragraphing and footnotes.

43

As modern technology has developed, Braille has turned out to be extraordinarily well-suited to computer-assisted production due to its elegance and efficiency. Braille displays for navigating and reading computer text in real time have become increasingly affordable and reliable as well. The computer age created an unprecedented and continuing explosion in the amount of Braille published and read in nearly every country throughout the world.

A. In spite of his blindness Louis attended his local school for some time, and was a bright student. Then when Louis was nine years old, his father entered into correspondence with the Minister of the Interior regarding whether it might be beneficial for Louis to attend the National Institute of the Blind in Paris. After lengthy consideration, Louis was nominated for attendance at the school.

B. Because it works, Braille has remained basically as Louis invented it. Nevertheless there have been some slight modification of the Braille system. A major goal has been to develop easily understood contractions representing groups of letters or whole words that appear frequently in a language. The use of contractions can make Braille books less cumbersome and permit even faster Braille reading.

C. Louis, inspired by the dedication of the Institute's founder, Valentin Hauy, and hungry for a more practical way to read, began searching for a new reading method. Nine years later, he had developed the basis for written communication for blind individuals that now carries his name – Braille.

D. Barbier's interest in fast, secret writing was grounded in his war experiences. Barbier had once seen all the troops in a forward-gun post annihilated when they betrayed their position by lighting a single lamp to read a message. A tactile system for sending and receiving messages could be useful not only at night, but in maintaining communications during combat with its unique horrors for artillery crews.

E. Then in 1812, when Louis was three years old, everything changed. Louis was playing in his father's workshop when an accident occurred that was to change his life forever and, consequently, the lives of visually impaired persons to this day. Legend has it that young Louis' hand slipped under the exertion of cutting a piece of leather, and the point of the tool, perhaps a knife or an awl, pierced his eye.

F. Today, Braille remains the foremost system of touch reading and writing for blind persons. It has been adapted for use in most all of the world's languages, including those that do not use the latin alphabet. The list of countries where it is used is very long.

G. But most importantly of all, Braille gives blind individuals access to a wide range of reading materials. This includes educational and recreational reading, financial statements, restaurant menus and practical manuals, not to mention the contracts, insurance policies and instructions that are part of daily adult life. Also, through Braille, blind people can pursue hobbies and cultural enrichment with such materials as music scores, playing cards and board games.

H. This original military code was called Night Writing and was used by soldiers to communicate after dark. It was based on a twelve-dot cell, two dots wide by six dots high. Each dot or combination of dots within the cell stood for a letter or a phonetic sound. The problem with the military code was that the human fingertip could not feel all the dots with one touch.

Paper 1 Reading   **PART 7**

You are going to read an extract from a book about creole languages. For questions 44 – 53, choose from the sections (A – E). The sections may be chosen more than once.

In which section are the following mentioned?

the reason why Jamaican Creole is looked down upon   **44**

a source by which Jamaicans were exposed to English after Patois developed   **45**

how most people speak in Jamaica   **46**

the name of the legally recognized language of Jamaica   **47**

why there are not many Arawaks in Jamaica today   **48**

the part of society that speaks the London Standard of English   **49**

the places where most Jamaican people live   **50**

a significant development during the years when growing sugar was important   **51**

African languages that were particularly important in the development of Patois   **52**

the characteristics that make Jamaican Patois unique   **53**

Creole Language in Jamaica

Language in Jamaica today reflects the history of the country's interaction with a variety of cultures and languages from many ethnic, linguistic, and social backgrounds. Aside from the Arawaks, the original inhabitants of Jamaica, all its people were exiles or children of exiles. Over 90% of the 2.5 million people living in Jamaica today are descendants of slaves brought from western Africa by the British. The local Jamaican language is a reflection of a history of contact with a variety of speakers, but the official language remains Standard English. The most influential speakers were immigrants from Africa and Europe. Kwa, Manding, and Kru are amongst the variety of prominent African languages apparent in Jamaican history. Early Modern English was brought to the Caribbean by sailors, soldiers, indentured servants, convicts, and lower-class settlers in the form of regional and non-standard dialects.

Today the Jamaican creole language, called Jamaican Patois, falls at one extreme of the linguistic spectrum while Standard English lies at the other end of the spectrum. The majority of the population speaks a language which falls in between the two. At one end there is the educated model spoken by the elite, which follows the "London Standard". At the other extreme is what linguists call "creolized" English, fragmented English speech and syntax with African influences developed during the days of slavery. This is the speech of the peasant or labourer with little education. In the middle of the language scale there is the inclusion of Jamaican rhythm and intonation of words, which evolved within the country, as well as the presence of other uniquely Jamaican traits including retention in common speech of English words now rare or poetic as well as new formations such as alterations of existing words.

Jamaican history and the formation of Patois are based on the experience of exile. In the early 16th century Spanish settlement began in Jamaica with the Arawaks as their first slave labour force. Within 100 years very few Arawaks survived due to a deadly epidemic. The only evidence of the Arawak dialect in Jamaica today is a few loan words, place names, food, natural objects, and events. Xaymaca is actually an Arawak word meaning "island of springs", which is where the name Jamaica is derived from. It is possible that the first contact of the Arawaks and the Spaniards may

have led to an early pidgin or bilingualism among the first generation of mixed blood. Throughout Spanish rule, the Arawaks had contact with Spanish colonists, Portuguese, Amerindians brought in as slaves from other parts of the Caribbean, and West Africans. Then in 1655 the English attacked the Spanish colony bringing with them new influences. Arriving with the invaders were soldiers recruited from England, Barbados, and Montserrat; settlers from Surinam, Barbados, Bermuda, New England, and Virginia; Jews from Brazil; indentured servants from Bristol; midland and northern lower-class English speakers; convicts from large prisons in England; Romany speakers; and a variety of African speakers. The birth of population centers, such as Port Royal, Passage Fort, and Kingston, served as a mixing pot of many different speakers.

Today linguists agree that East Indians, Spanish, and Arawaks have contributed a little vocabulary to the Jamaican dialect, but the majority of non-English terms, grammar and phonology is African. Africans came to acquire forms of English because of the domination of the English dialects of their plantation-owning masters. The heyday of sugar, between 1700-1834, is the period thought to be most responsible for the forming of Patois. At this time, increasing numbers of Africans were imported to work on the large plantations. By the end of the century Africans made up a quarter of the slave population and Creole took precedence over the African past. Increases in written records of Jamaican Creole were seen during the abolitionist movement in 1770 to 1838 but English continued to influence Jamaican Creole in the form of biblical language and prayer book language.

The perception that English-lexicon Creole languages are a form of "bad English" still persists today in Jamaica. Jamaican Patois continues to be considered an unacceptable official language and an informal language not to be used for any formal purpose. Creole speakers are often compared to those speakers of Standard English. The similarity of Creole to English has led Creole speakers to be labelled as socially and linguistically inferior, although Jamaica Creole is increasingly showing up in newspapers once known for their old-fashioned Standard English, on the radio, and in songs. Indeed, in the past 30 or 40 years linguists have finally begun to recognize Creole as a language in itself.

PART 1

Read the two texts below.

Write an essay summarising and evaluating the key points from both texts. Use your own words throughout as far as possible, and include your own ideas in your answer.

Write your answer in **240 - 280 words**.

Lying is Part of Life

Honesty, we say, is the best policy. And yet, it's hardly news to anyone that in much of our lives, dishonesty rules. Salespeople lie about the benefits of one product over another, partners lie about whether they liked dinner and, of course, politicians lie about the colour of the sky and the existence of stones. We look down on dishonesty, yet we lie all the time. We all know that "little white lies" are a kind of social lubricant, making everything run that much more smoothly. Why have a fight when it's so much easier just to say what the other person wants to hear?

The Cost of Lying

The problem with lying is it is a short term gain, which increases the likelihood of long-term pain. Others, of course, learn who lies to them and who does not, and they will have no respect for you if they know you lie. That is a very big burden for you to carry. When you lie, you are behaving without integrity, and that is very very expensive for you because it costs you your self-respect. If you do not want to tell the truth to someone, that is absolutely fine; they cannot demand you tell them more than you wish to say, but lying is not the way to get around telling the truth.

Write your **essay**.

Paper 2 WRITING **PART 2**

PART 2

Write an answer to **one** of the questions **2 - 4** in this part. Write your answer in **280 - 320** words, in an appropriate style, in the space provided on the next page. .Put the question number in the box on the top of page where you will write your answer.

2. You belong to an English-language film club where you recently saw a film in 3D. You have agreed to write a **review** of this film for the group's monthly news letter. In this review you should give your opinion of the 3D effects in the film and say whether you think 3D adds anything, in general, to the experience of watching a movie.

Write your **review**.

3. Your local newspaper has published a story about plans to develop one of the parks near your home. The trees will be cleared and a small shopping centre and parking lot will be built on the land. You decide to send a **letter** to the editor of the newspaper expressing your opinions on this matter and addressing the likely effects that this development will have on your community in the short and longer terms.

Write your **letter.**

4. Your teacher has recently caught some students cheating on exams. He is upset and disappointed and has asked you to talk to your fellow students and write a report about students' views on cheating. He wants to find out about why students would cheat, what would be a fitting punishment for cheating, and what could be done to discourage this behaviour in the future.

Write your **report.**

Listening Exam Practice

Paper 3 LISTENING | **PART 1**

You will hear three different extracts
For questions 1 - 6, choose the answer (A, B or C) which fits best according to what you hear.
There are two questions for each extract.

Extract One

You hear a teacher speaking about working with autistic children.

1. What does the speaker say about the general perception of autism?
   A. Her experience supports it.
   B. It can be misleading.
   C. It was created by teachers.

2. The speaker implies that autistic children
   A. could be taught better.
   B. can communicate verbally.
   C. do not enjoy life.

Extract Two

You hear a man and woman discussing endangered languages in the United States.

3. What do the speakers agree about?
   A. The statistic is not what they expected.
   B. The statistic is not accurate.
   C. The statistic is unbelievable.

4. What is the woman's outlook on the situation?
   A. Little can be done.
   B. Everyone recognises the problem.
   C. It is not hopeless.

Extract Three

You hear a professor talking about getting reactions from his students.

5. What is the professor's opinion about surveys?
   A. They are less useful than his colleagues think.
   B. They are a complete waste of time.
   C. They cannot elicit a response from students.

6. The professor implies that his students
   A. are reluctant to communicate.
   B. need feedback on their performance.
   C. know he values their opinions.

Paper 3 LISTENING | PART 2

You will hear a researcher talking about communication in the environmental science fields, and how communication on environmental issues could be improved.
For questions 7 - 15, complete the sentence with a word or a short phrase.

There is a deep cultural view that knowledge leads people to do **7** _____ .

However, to solve environmental problems, obstacles must also be **8** _____ .

The idea that knowledge automatically leads to the correct behaviour is too **9** _____ .

People are now convinced of climate change but don't know about the **10** _____ .

Martin Luther King was effective because he gave people a message of **11** _____ .

Hard work and luck might produce warming at the **12** _____ of future projections.

We will see negative change in the environment in spite of **13** _____ .

Though those living today will see only climate **14** _____ they may see positive social change.

It is important to sustain people's **15** _____ in working towards a better climate.

Paper 3 LISTENING | PART 3

You will hear a theoretical biologist, Dr Nowak, being interviewed by a colleague about the evolution of language. For questions 16 - 20, choose the answer (A, B, C or D) which fits best according to what you hear.

16 Dr Nowak is seeking to
   A. create a new branch of science.
   B. change his specialty.
   C. combine disparate fields.
   D. recruit theoretical biologists.

17 Dr Nowak jokes that mathematical biologists
   A. know little about the real world.
   B. are not as clever as shepherds.
   C. covet other people's possessions.
   D. don't see well.

18 Why does the subject of language evolution attract Dr Nowak?
   A. It is forbidden.
   B. It was studied by famous people.
   C. It is virtually unexplored.
   D. It is complex and controversial.

19 What point is made about the significance of the evolution of language?
   A. It is important because it is the most recent event.
   B. It is unimportant compared to that of the nervous system
   C. It actually changed the rules of evolution.
   D. It is the most significant evolutionary step of all.

20 The evolution of language has made what possible?
   A. culture
   B. cultural evolution
   C. the transfer of information in a different way
   D. the transfer of information across generations

You will hear five short extracts in which different people are talking about a time when they were saved by their mobile phone. You will hear the recording twice. While you listen, you must complete both tasks.

TASK ONE

For questions, 21 - 25 choose from the list (A - H) what each speaker was doing at the time of the incident they describe.

A surfing

B reporting from a war zone

C walking alone at night

D hang gliding

E kayaking

F fighting a battle

G traveling home intoxicated

H skiing

TASK TWO

For questions 26 - 30, choose from the list (A - H) how each person's phone helped him or her.

A transmitted a location to rescuers

B got important news to a relative

C broke a fall

D alerted paramedics

E reported a crime to authorities

F prevented a gunshot wound

G discouraged a possible attacker

H provided a diversion

Speaker 1	21
Speaker 2	22
Speaker 3	23
Speaker 4	24
Speaker 5	25

Speaker 1	26
Speaker 2	27
Speaker 3	28
Speaker 4	29
Speaker 5	30